THE PRESENT

ANDREA TORREY BALSARA

THE PRESENT

ANDREA TORREY BALSARA

Pearson Australia
(a division of Pearson Australia Group Pty Ltd)
707 Collins Street, Melbourne, Victoria 3008
PO Box 23360, Melbourne, Victoria 8012
www.pearson.com.au

ISBN: 978-1-86970-643-2

Produced by Pearson

Commissioning Editor: Lucy Armour
Editors: Elizabeth Hookings, Jan Chilwell
Page Layout and Design: Sarah Healey

Printed in Australia by the SOS Print + Media Group

Pearson Australia Group Pty Ltd   ABN 40 004 245 943

AUTHOR NOTE

A couple of years ago I heard someone refer to "the emotional abandonment of children" and it got me thinking. When I think of an abandoned child, images of gaunt street children come to mind. Emotional abandonment was something I had never thought of before: parents too busy with their careers, or single parents working day and night to keep food on the table; parents so overwhelmed with their own emotional lives that they have nothing left to give, even to their child.

Originally, when I began to write *The Present*, I thought the theme would be emotional abandonment, and it is. But the story evolved into something else as well. It also became a story about being human: making horrible mistakes and finding forgiveness and love.

Andrea Torrey Balsara

Rudy is a stupid name for a dog, don't you think? But that's the one he came with. My dad gave him to me for my fourteenth birthday. A weird boxer-golden retriever mix with a mashed face and a furry tail.

It was the last week in June, just before the summer holiday. All my friends were at my pool for my birthday party – I think we were playing water volleyball or something like that – when my mum said, "Julie, it's time to open presents." As if I was four and not fourteen. She stood there with a big smile on her face, holding a present.

"It's okay, Mum, I'll open them later," I said. "We're just hanging out for now."

The smile on my mum's face disappeared. Then my friends started hauling themselves out of the pool.

"Come on, Jules," said Megan. She knows what Mum can be like. We've been best friends since day care.

Suddenly, there was this crash, and a loud *WOOF!*

Jessica Striker shrieked. "Omigawwd, it's a DOG!" (Dogs scare the you-know-what out of her because one bit her when she was five, or something. She still has the scar on her cheek.)

And then I saw my dad with this strange-looking mutt on a leash, coming into the backyard. The dog was straining so hard its tongue was purple and its eyes bulged. So did my dad's as he tried to hold it back.

My mum stood there, holding that present, with a look on her face like she smelled something bad.

"Charlie. What the . . . ?"

Dad hauled the dog over, handed me the leash and collapsed into a deckchair.

"He's all yours. Name's Rudy. Happy birthday, baby." He rubbed his hand over his face. "I need a beer."

My mum gasped. *"He's . . . What . . .?"* She was speechless. Then her voice came back just fine. "Are you out of your mind? Don't you think I might want to know if we're getting a dog, especially such a hideous, old, slobbery . . ."

"It's okay, Mum," I interrupted. "I love him."

"Julie, this is between your father and me," she snapped.

"Back off, Claire," said my dad. "I know he's butt-ugly, but this guy at work wanted to get rid of him. You know, I was thinking about how much Julie wants a dog, so I took him. But of course all you want to do is nag and complain . . ."

"This present was from us!" She held the forlorn-looking present out to him and shook it. "*Remember?*" She started to cry. "Why did I even bother getting something? You always do this to me . . ."

"How can I always do this to you when I've never brought home a dog before? I try to do something nice . . . You know what? Forget it! I'm going out." My dad jerked himself out of the deckchair and stalked back around the house.

Mum ran after him. "You come back here! I won't let you ruin Julie's party!" She was still shouting when we heard my dad's engine rev. Tyres squealed and then there was silence.

My friends stared, wide-eyed, like they were watching a horror movie. Megan, her boyfriend Kevin, Jessica, Samantha, Suze, Brianna.

There was a pounding in my ears. It felt like the whole ocean was in my head, crashing against my skull.

I rolled my eyes and laughed. It sounded more like a cough. I said, "It's so hard to raise parents these days." That sounded lame, even to me. Nobody laughed.

Then Megan said, "Last one in the pool's a rotten egg," and broke the spell. Everyone kind of shook it off and the pounding fell away . . .

I'd forgotten about Rudy, but just then he lunged, ripping his leash out of my hand. He sailed into the pool, doing a perfect belly flop.

I think Rudy's a smart dog. I have trained him to sit and stay. I just hold out my hand and say, "Stay," and he does. If I want him to come, I just slap my hand on my chest (I borrowed a training video from the library) and say in a loud, commanding voice, "COME." And he does. It's pretty cool.

Two days after my party, my dad left my mum. I guess I wasn't surprised, but I was still surprised, you know what I mean? Like when you feel something bad is coming, but when it does you're thinking, "Wow, I can't believe it!" It took my mum by surprise, too.

I remember sitting out on the grass in the backyard and hearing them.

"Who is she?"

"Why does there have to be anybody else when you're such a . . ."

"When I'm such a . . . And what about you? You are so . . ."

Clouds moved lazily across the sky. Even though it was only the beginning of summer, it was hot. A bug sang on a nearby tree – a cicada, I think it was. Had a sound like a drill boring holes in the thick air.

"Evie. Her name is Evie! There! You happy?"

"I knew it! I knew it! I knew . . ."

Rudy put his big, heavy head on my leg. His fur prickled my bare skin, but I didn't mind. I scratched behind his ears and he groaned and drooled on my leg. One of the clouds was shaped like a dog. I swear.

The moving van pulled up, gears grinding as it shuddered to a stop. My dad got out with one of his mates (Dave? Bobby? Can't remember) and walked over to the pile of junk in the middle of our lawn. I watched from behind my curtain in my bedroom. Rudy sat by my side, panting. His slobber dripped on my foot.

Dad was shaking his head. "That woman never lets up, does she?" He kicked a baseball mitt lying on top of the stack and it flew off and slapped against my window. *THUNK!* I stepped back from the window.

"*YOU NEVER LET UP, DO YOU, CLAIRE?*" he yelled at the house.

"Julie, come here. I need help carrying out your father's junk!" My mum's voice was shrill. I ignored her. "JULIE, WHERE ARE YOU?"

Suddenly, the door swung open. Mum was standing there. I could see her lips moving, but, honest to God, I couldn't hear anything. The ocean in my head was there again.

I could see she was mad. She was holding a pile of my dad's T-shirts. She was holding them out to me, shaking them. I knew she wanted me to take them, but my arms felt so heavy.

"Here, take them. *TAKE THEM!*" Her shouts reached me and my arms stretched out. They looked like naked branches on a tree.

Rudy jumped up and pushed by my mum, almost knocking her off her feet. The T-shirts cascaded like falling leaves onto the floor.

"Hey, you . . ." she said. But Rudy was already gone.

I looked through the window. Now Rudy was in the front yard, galloping back and forth as my dad and Dave or Bobby loaded stuff into the van.

Too late, I saw Rudy sniffing around the pile of junk. He lifted his leg and shot a stream of bright yellow pee at a pile of underwear and socks.

"Stupid dog!" bellowed my dad, red-faced. He threw a CD at Rudy and caught him on the haunch.

Rudy yelped and ran.

High-pitched laughter came from another part of the house. "Good boy!" gurgled Mum. At least she and Rudy were finally bonding.

The family circus eventually moved to the next town, and all the curious neighbours, rubberneckers and people-who-were-shocked went back inside their houses. It was just me, my mum and Rudy.

And a really big, empty house.

Actually, it wasn't empty, it was pretty messy. There were socks, underwear, shirts and stuff lying all over (my dad's), scattered car magazines and various books (my dad's), plant dirt where Mum had tossed out plants Dad had given her.

It just *felt* empty.

There was a smell in the air: roasting chicken. Someone next door must be having roast chicken. They would cook it, maybe make a salad, pour milk or juice for drinks, and everyone would sit down together and eat.

Rudy looked at me and, I swear, his eyes were full of tears.

CHAPTER TWO

I can't remember the first day after my dad left. Maybe you don't believe me, but it's true. I must have eaten something, I must have slept, because I wasn't starving or sleep-deprived when I finally came to.

I don't know if my dad phoned. I don't know if any of my friends phoned, either. (Mum wasn't in the mood to take messages, if you know what I mean.) I hope they did.

After I snapped out of it, I rang my dad's cellphone, but there was no answer. Tried to phone Megan, too. Her mum said she was out with Kevin and could she give me a ring when she comes back? I said sure.

There was no noise from my mum's room, although there were empty Chinese takeaway cartons on the coffee table so I knew she was probably around somewhere.

I took Rudy out for a long walk, just the two of us. We went down along the river. Thin strands of river grass were combed over the mud where the river had overflowed its banks. That's where we walked, our feet sinking into the sandy mud.

Rudy's paw print was almost as big as my foot.

Old coffee cups and plastic bags clung against the reeds higher up the bank. Rudy sniffed every blade of river grass and reed and, if they really smelled good, he peed on them.

It was nice being out. We walked back down our street and stopped at Jessica's house. She lives three houses down.

I rang the bell and her dad opened the door. Mr Striker is a maths teacher at my school. He's nice, I guess, but he speaks so slowly. I actually do a very funny imitation of him. It cracks Megan up (I don't do it around Jessica). "Uh . . . class . . . uh . . . open your books to . . . uh . . . page three . . . uh . . ."

"Hi, Mr Striker," I said. "Is Jessica home?"

"Hello, Julie. Uh . . . no, she's out with her . . . mum." He stepped out onto the porch and bent his head down towards me as if what he was going to say was top secret. "Uh . . . Julie," he said in a low voice, "I heard about your family's . . . uh . . . troubles . . ."

"Oh yeah?" I said. I took a step back and crunched

Rudy's paw. He yelped loudly. "Sorry, Rudy," I said.

"Rudy, eh?" Mr Striker leaned over and scratched Rudy behind the ears. "Hello, Rudy. Nice to . . . uh . . . meet you." He kept scratching. Rudy groaned and leaned against Mr Striker's leg.

Then Mr Striker looked back up at me. His forehead creased up into rows of concerned wrinkles. "Julie, I . . . uh . . . want you to know how . . . uh . . . sorry we all are." Rudy licked his hand. "Good boy . . . so . . . uh . . . how are you doing?" He stopped scratching and looked straight into my eyes.

His eyes were blue with tiny flecks of gold. I'd never noticed that before.

I couldn't say anything. My tongue felt thick lying in my mouth. As if it was a log or a stone or something. I just nodded and shrugged.

His eyes looked so sad. I nodded again and tried to smile. The edges of my mouth began to shake with the effort, but just then Rudy collapsed on the welcome mat and rolled onto his back, showing his belly, so I don't think Mr Striker saw.

He knelt and scratched Rudy's belly until the dog moaned with pleasure, his eyes half-closed. Then Mr Striker looked up at me and smiled. "You're . . . uh . . . a good kid, Julie . . . I know that . . . uh . . . things will turn out . . . uh . . . okay for you."

I cried walking home. I don't know why. But for once Rudy didn't strain at the leash, which was a good thing.

When I opened the door to the house there was no sign of Mum. No new takeaway containers, either. I knocked on her door.

"Mum?" There was a rustling sound. "Mum? You in there?"

No answer. I put my head around the door. She was lying crossways, face up, over the king-size bed, still in her pyjamas. She had makeup stains running down her cheeks and a snot bubble that went in and out with her soft snores.

I wiped her nose (got a little snot on me, which was gross, but I washed my hands afterwards) and tucked the quilt over her. Then I crept out, shutting the door behind me.

"Come on, Rudy," I whispered. "I'll make you a feast."

I made myself some peanut butter toast and a few pieces for Rudy, too. It's actually one of my favourite things to eat, so that was fine. Rudy gulped it down then sat smacking his lips, trying to get the peanut butter to go down.

The sun was setting, shining through the sliding doors in the kitchen. Rudy and I sat on the couch in the living room, with the lights out. Sometimes I like it better that way, you know? More relaxing. I could hear the clock ticking on the wall.

I got the phone and dialled Megan's number.

"Is Megan there?" I asked Mrs Bartlet.

"Is that Julie? She's not here, honey. She had to go out again, but she told me she'll try to phone you later, okay? Are you going to be at home, dear?"

I looked around the living room. "Yeah, I guess. Thanks."

"That's okay, honey. And Julie?"

Oh no. "Yes, Mrs Bartlet?"

"I'm sorry about your mum and dad, honey. Really sorry."

"Thanks . . . Bye."

"Bye now."

That stupid clock was really getting on my nerves. I turned on the TV to drown it out, but nothing good was on. There was a boring dance contest with famous people, some kind of debate with really boring people, a boring movie that I'd already seen and didn't ever want to see again.

I flipped the channels so much that Rudy looked up at me and whined. I don't blame him. It would bug me, too, if someone else was doing it. He kept staring at me, so I turned the TV off and he laid his head down, smacking his lips.

I picked up the phone and tried to ring my dad again. I thought, you know, maybe he had finished moving in and now he could answer the phone. But it rang and rang and no one picked it up.

I am standing on top of a mountain and the view is amazing. I can breathe here. I fill my lungs and I smell clean snow, wild meadow flowers, fresh, tangy air. There are mountains everywhere and the sky is so blue. I make the mistake of looking down and see an ocean far below. The water is thick and black. Suddenly, the ocean starts to whirl, like ink going down a drain. I try to stay still, but where I'm standing is all loose rock. My feet scramble, but the stones roll out from under me and my legs fail. I fall towards the swirling ink. There is a ringing in my ears . . . the ocean rushes to meet me . . . ringing . . .

"Finally!" It was Megan. "Did you go out or something?"

"No," I said, holding the phone to my ear. My hand was kind of shaky. I didn't even remember picking up the phone. "I was here. I . . . I was just . . . I must have fallen asleep. Sorry."

"That's cool," she said. "I just got back from my date. You wanna hear about it?" She giggled.

"I . . . Maybe tomorrow, okay? I'm feeling kind of . . . you know."

"Oh," she said. "Yeah. How are you? I'm sorry I haven't phoned, but I thought you might want some space. I know I would if I were you."

"Yeah, thanks. I'm . . . um . . ." I tried to focus. "I'm okay. Just hanging out."

"Cool. You want to come over tomorrow? Kevin is helping his dad with some stupid thing at work so I'm not doing anything. And my mum said you can bring your dog. What's his name again?"

"Rudy," I said. "Yeah, that'd be great. I'll get there somehow. Maybe I'll ride my bike." Mum usually drove me, but I really wanted to see Megan and I didn't think Mum would be driving me anywhere right then.

After I hung up, I brushed my teeth and got into my pyjamas. I went to get into bed, but Rudy had got there first and was sprawled across it. He was blinking up at me, all innocent. I pushed him and he snorted at me, but finally moved over.

I slept with my back against his and didn't have any more dreams that I can remember.

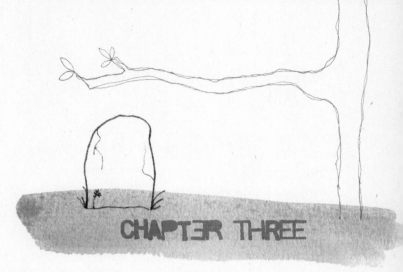

CHAPTER THREE

When I got up the next morning, Mum was gone. So was her car. Probably she'd gone to work or something. She works at a bank. She's the manager.

The dishes in the sink were starting to smell, so I did them. I wiped down the table and swept the kitchen floor. I had to – everywhere I stepped, crumbs or something crunched under my feet and I really hate that.

I got a bowl and spoon and poured out some cereal for myself. Rudy stared at me with a you-never-feed-me look. "Yeah, yeah," I said. "You can wait." I got the milk out of the fridge, but when I put some on my cereal, I swear, it came out in chunks.

"Gee, you think it's bad or something, Rudy?" I asked him. He tilted his head at me and sniffed. "What do you say to peanut butter toast again?" He panted at me – it looked like he was smiling.

So I guess that meant yes.

I dumped the cereal and made us both some toast.

Rudy was still smacking his lips when we finally got going. I'd had to pump up my tyres and get a long piece of rope so he could run next to me. First thing he did was lunge in front of the bike, but then he sort of got the hang of it.

We rode for about ten minutes and I saw all sorts of things I normally didn't even notice. I never rode that far usually. I was staring at an old graveyard on top of a big hill when I drove my bike into a ditch. Rudy landed on top of me and knocked the wind right out of me. We both sat there for a minute, just breathing. But nothing was broken, so we kept going.

"Come on, Rudy," I called, teetering on my bike, trying to stay upright. Rudy pulled on the leash, and I was about to take another header. "Rudy, heel!" But Rudy plunged ahead. We needed to go over what "heel" meant, I guess.

We finally got to Megan's. I tried to stop, but Rudy kept going and I kind of crashed into the garage door. Luckily, it didn't hurt too much and Rudy stood there panting at me with a smile on his face.

"Oh ha, ha, ha," I said.

Mrs Bartlet answered when I knocked. She was like one of those mothers you see in the movies, you know what I mean? Her cheeks looked like two red apples and her short dark hair was a mass of soft curls. She was wearing an apron and was just taking off oven mitts. A buttery, baking smell wafted out the door.

"Julie, come in! It's so good to see you, dear." She held open the door. "Megan's just on the phone, but did you want to try some of my biscuits? Come and sit down and I'll get you a plate." She bustled off.

I hesitated because I didn't know what to do with Rudy. She must have felt it through the walls or something, because she called from the kitchen. "And, honey, don't be shy about bringing in your dog. This house has seen worse, believe me!" So we both walked right in.

Rudy sank onto the carpet and fell asleep instantly. The run must have really worn him out if he could sleep through the smell of those biscuits.

I drank milk and crunched sugar biscuits – I don't know how many. She kept bringing them, so I figured she must have enough. After I had eaten maybe a hundred, Megan finally came out of her room and hugged me.

"I've missed you, Jules," she said.

We sat on Megan's bed. Rudy was snoring loudly next to it. He'd dragged himself to Megan's room when we went in there and immediately dropped into a coma again.

"So how's it been?" she asked, leaning with her back against the wall, making a thick ponytail of her hair. She's got long black hair that always looks good.

I shrugged and stared up at the ceiling. "Did you know you've got a crack that goes all the way along the wall?"

Megan shrugged, too. "Who cares?" She put an elastic band on her ponytail and tossed it over her shoulder. "That crack's been there for ages. It's not growing or anything."

"I'd be afraid it would break open and the ceiling would fall on me in the middle of the night or something."

"I never thought about it," she said. "But now I will. Thanks a lot, Jules."

I laughed. "No problem."

We sat there saying nothing for a while. Then she said, "How's your mum taking it?"

"I don't know. Okay, I guess. She's been sleeping a lot."

She chewed her lip. "Kevin was right. You know, he could tell something was really wrong at the party.

I snorted. "What tipped him off?" I said. "My mum screaming or my dad taking off?"

Megan glared at me. "His parents divorced when he was three. He's been through a lot, too, Julie."

"Sorry," I said. "I didn't mean . . . " My voice trailed off.

Megan stared at the wall, her chin stuck out like a prizefighter's. She does that when she's really mad. "I mean," she said, shaking her head, "he was only trying to help, and you know . . ." She kept shaking her head. I waited for her to finish her sentence.

"Sorry," I finally said again. She kept staring at the wall and shaking her head. I played with the pink flower things sewn onto her bedspread, but nobody said anything else.

The silence was suddenly broken when Rudy did a giant yawn and hauled himself to his feet. He stretched right in front of Megan, his back legs quivering.

I saw his stomach lurch.

"Rudy, NO!" I yelled. It lurched again.

Megan's eyes were round with horror. She pulled her legs up, but she was too late. Rudy did a giant heave and peanut butter-coloured puke spewed all over Megan's feet and across her pink-flowered bedspread.

She screamed like she was being attacked by an axe murderer.

"YOU STUPID DOG. WHAT IS YOUR PROBLEM?" (Mrs Bartlet must have gone out for a minute, because if she was in the house she would have heard for sure.) Megan leaped off the bed, dripping, still shouting at poor Rudy. No wonder he hadn't wanted any biscuits.

"He couldn't help it," I said. "I mean, I'm sure he didn't try to do it." Just then Rudy burped and a huge gob of drool dribbled out the side of his mouth and onto her carpet. Megan looked at him as if he was a steaming pile of you-know-what. Then she turned her gaze on me.

"Julie, get a clue," she said and walked out of the room, slamming the door shut behind her.

I'm riding home. I see trees go by. Cars go by, but I can't hear them. All I hear are the pounding waves.

I see Rudy running next to me – running in slow motion. Everything is in slow motion. A long, black

line snakes beside me. I fly over the edge of it and fall
. . . but I don't scream.

My bike wheel was still spinning when I came to. Rudy was licking my face. My head ached.

I looked around. I was sitting at the bottom of a deep ditch. Cars were whizzing by, but no one could see me, I guess. It was a pretty deep ditch.

Rudy whined and pawed at my leg. I scratched behind his ears, but my hand was shaking so I dropped it and rested my head against his side. "It's okay, boy. It's going to be okay." He was so warm.

I dug my fingers into his fur and cried.

When I finally hauled my bike out of the ditch, I saw we were near the old graveyard on the hill. Rudy and I walked over there (he walked beside me nicely the whole way; I was really surprised) and we looked around. The gravestones were bleached out and dry-looking, as if they were bones themselves. The words were hard to make out on some of them, they'd been there for so long.

Up on top of the hill, under a massive tree, one little marker rose crookedly out of the ground. Its words were outlined with that kind of moss that grows on rocks, whatever it's called. Maybe the tree protected it from the rain because its letters were really clear.

Here Lies Our Beloved Daughter
Elizabeth Ellen Main.
Born September 9, 1854.
Died November 13, 1856.
"Only a Short Time on Earth,
But in Our Hearts Forever."

Rudy sat quietly as I read it out loud to him. Elizabeth was only two when she died. Nearby were her parents' gravestones. The mother had died in 1870, the father in 1874. "At least they're all together now," I said to Rudy. He sniffed.

I wondered what Elizabeth had been like. Did she have blonde or brown hair, or red even? Was she chubby? Had she been sickly her whole life (all two years of it)? I wondered how her mum and dad had felt when she died.

Do you ever think of things like that, or is it just me? I mean, it's as if I saw this little family all together, being so happy, and then one day – boom – she's gone.

I felt pretty sad all the way home. And even though Rudy cut in front of the bike and I almost fell again I didn't yell at him.

We got home just after dark. My mum's car was in the driveway. I put my bike in the garage and opened the front door. I kept Rudy close to me. He was looking tired and I didn't want him doing anything stupid.

"Mum?" I called. The house was dark and quiet.

"Hi." My mum was sitting on the couch. I hadn't even seen her. I must have jumped, because Mum said, "What's the matter, Julie? You look as if you've seen a ghost." She didn't move.

"Mum, are you okay?" I don't know why, but my heart was pounding. Like, why would I be afraid of my own mum? But I was. Rudy leaned against my leg, so I think he was a little scared, too.

Mum gave a dry laugh. "Never better, Julie, never better. Sit down," she said, pointing to the end of the couch.

I stayed standing. "Um, Mum," I said. "We kind of need more milk and food and things. I . . . I had to feed Rudy peanut butter for two days and he . . . he just threw it up. So maybe could you buy some . . . dog food or something?"

There was an unpleasant silence. I could feel her stare boring through me like a drill. When she spoke, her voice was low. "Julie, I will buy you whatever food you want. Milk, eggs . . . whatever you need."

Her voice cut into me. "But I . . . won't . . . buy . . . that . . . dog . . . a . . . thing."

I gulped back the tears. I walked towards my room like a wooden marionette, with Rudy behind me. One foot in front of the other . . . one foot in front of the other . . . one foot . . .

"Julie," she said.

I stopped. I did not turn around.

"Your father rang. I told him you weren't here. He didn't leave a message."

CHAPTER FOUR

I lay in bed long after the sun came up, and then I only got up because Rudy was whining and scratching at the door. I grabbed a T-shirt off the floor and a pair of shorts and put them on.

Out in the hall I saw Mum's door was open, but the room was empty.

I took Rudy to the sliding doors and let him outside. There was a twenty-dollar note on the table with a piece of paper under it.

Julie, can you pick up a few things for dinner?
I'll be home around 5.30.
Mum
P.S. I need to talk to you about last night.

I stared at the note for a moment, then stuffed it in my pocket.

I picked up the phone and rang Dad's number. No answer again. I stared at the phone in my hand. I wanted to smash it against the wall, but I laid it carefully back in its holder instead.

Rudy whined at the door, so I let him in and looked in the fridge for something to eat. There was a pot of something with a plate on top. I took it out, but whatever it was had grown green fuzzy mould. (It must have shot out some spores, or whatever they're called, because I started sneezing.)

There was one wrinkly apple in the fruit bowl, so I washed it, cut it in two and tossed half to Rudy (he was sitting next to me, staring). He caught it mid-air and gulped it down.

I was going to eat the other half, but he kept on staring so I tossed him that, too. He caught it and swallowed without even chewing and stared at me again.

My stomach was still rumbling, so I looked in the cupboard for more food. There was some instant rice, so I cooked that up.

I'd never had rice for breakfast before, but it wasn't too bad. Rudy seemed to like it okay – he licked his bowl and let out a gigantic burp. In fact, he looked so pleased with himself, I laughed, even though I didn't really feel like it.

There were mountains of dishes everywhere. And there was laundry, too. Maybe I would do it when I got back.

Rudy and I set off for the shops. It wasn't far. Maybe a five-minute walk or so. He kept pulling on the leash until his tongue was purple (which kind of reminded me of the day he arrived, at the party – not too great).

"Heel, Rudy," I said, jerking the leash up and towards me, the way the library video showed me, but he lunged again. "Heel!" We did that all the way to the shops, until my wrist ached.

"You know what I don't get, Rudy?" I said, as I leaned over him to tie his leash to the shop railing. He panted in my face, smiling. "Why are you so good sometimes and so bad other times?" He kept panting and smiling, all the way up until I stepped into the shop. Then he screeched like he'd been abandoned or something.

All the way through the shop I could hear Rudy howling.

"My goodness," one old lady said to me. "What on earth is making that racket? Is that someone's *dog*?" I just shrugged and shook my head, as if I was just as disgusted as she was.

I walked faster, dumping things into my basket.

Eggs . . . bread . . . butter . . . milk . . . a bag of apples
. . . I stopped dead in front of the dog food. A happy
collie dog smiled out at me. *"Doesn't Your Best Friend
Deserve the Very Best?"* the bag declared. It was $4.20
for a small bag. Almost a quarter of my budget. Just
then, Rudy howled extra loud (it was as if he could
read my mind or something) and that decided it. I
put the bag in the basket. I would worry about what
to tell Mum later.

I got into the "Twelve Items or Less" lane. The
guy in front of me put his stuff on the conveyor (he
had fourteen items, but what was I going to say?)
while I tried to add up what I was buying. When I
got to the bag of dog food, I got this kind of knot in
my stomach. It was going to be tight.

The guy paid and left and the lady on the till said
to me, "Good morning, dear." I smiled, but my lips
felt a little shaky, so I didn't say anything. Rudy must
have caught sight of me, because he was staring
at me through the window. His breath fogged up
the glass.

"Is he yours?" asked the cashier. Just then Rudy
gave a piercing, high-pitched yowl. I nodded.

"He's kind of cute," she said. "And he sure seems
to love you a lot, doesn't he?"

I looked at Rudy, who was yowling so much I

swear I could see foam on the sides of his mouth. "Yeah," I said. "I guess he does."

She finished ringing up my stuff and smiled at me. "That'll be $22.93, dear."

My cheeks got hot. I handed her the twenty. "That's all I've got," I said. "Just take out the butter or something." I grabbed the butter and held it out to her, my hand shaking a little.

She glanced around, as if she didn't want anyone to hear, and leaned towards me. "Don't worry about it," she said. She took the butter from me and put it back in the bag. "Don't you worry about it at all."

"But I . . ."

"I'll pay for it, don't you worry."

"Thank you," I said, trying to smile, tears prickling behind my eyes. I fumbled at the bags and she handed them to me.

"You take care, dear." Then she stood and watched me leave, like a mummy sending her child off on the school bus.

When I untied Rudy, he acted as if I'd left him there for a year, jumping up at me and licking my face, but before we walked home I kneeled and gave him a huge hug. He got really still and put his head on my shoulder and we just sat there for a minute.

Somehow I got the bags and Rudy home. It wasn't easy. Mum still wasn't home, so I put down a bowl of dog food for Rudy and he kind of dived at it, as if he was starving or something (I guess he really doesn't like peanut butter). Then I hid the dog food.

I cleaned the dishes, wiped the table, swept and mopped the kitchen floor. I did the laundry and folded the clothes. I vacuumed up the dirt and stuff in the living room. It looked really good when I was finished. Then I took Rudy to the backyard and I worked on something with him for the rest of the afternoon.

By the time Mum got home, I had made scrambled eggs, had bread toasting and a plate of sliced apples on the table for dessert.

Mum looked tired when she came in, but when she smelled the toast it must have made her feel good, because she smiled.

"We're having scrambled eggs and toast," I said.

Mum didn't say anything. She looked around the living room, then she walked into the kitchen. She shook her head as if she couldn't believe it. "Julie, you must have worked all day on this."

I pulled out a chair from the table for her and she sat down slowly, still looking around her. I guess she was really surprised.

The toast shot up in the toaster, so I buttered it and stacked the pieces on a plate. I spooned the scrambled eggs onto a serving dish and put it out on the table, with plates and cutlery. Mum just sat there, kind of touching her knife and fork like they had turned into gold or something.

"Would you like milk or water?" I asked her.

"Umm . . . milk, please," she said, still looking like she was in the wrong house.

The whole time Rudy sat restlessly by the couch. When I looked his way, he stood up and his eyes seemed to be saying, "Can I come and eat, too? Can I? I'm starving, you know . . ." I held out my hand and stared him down. He slunk back onto his haunches.

Mum and I ate our eggs (they were actually pretty good) and our toast. She didn't say much, but I could tell she really liked everything.

When we had finished, she took my hand. Her head was bent over so that I couldn't see her face. I saw a couple of tears plop onto the table.

"I'm sorry, Julie," she said. Her voice was thick. "I'm so sorry." I squeezed her hand and she pulled me in, hugging me to her. I could feel her body shaking. We held on to each other for a long time.

I felt something bump against me. Rudy had put

his head on Mum's knee. She let go of me and stared at him. She didn't look mad or upset, just kind of bewildered. Sort of like, who is this dog and why is he putting his head on my knee, you know?

I stroked Rudy's head. "It's okay, Mum. He can tell you're sad, so he wants to make you feel better."

Mum reached out her hand and slowly scratched him behind his ears. Rudy groaned. "He likes it, Mum," I said. "He likes you."

Mum pulled back her hand, her face suddenly hard.

"Um, Mum, look what he can do. I worked with him on it all afternoon!" I said quickly. "Rudy!" I held out my fingers as if they were a gun. "Bang!" Rudy dropped to his side and rolled onto his back, his four legs sticking up in the air like road kill.

Even though she didn't want to, Mum laughed. I got Rudy to do it again and again. "Bang!" Each time he'd drop like a rock and poke his legs in the air. Mum couldn't stop laughing. "Bang!" "Bang!" We both laughed until we cried.

"Enough, enough," she said, holding her side. "Oh, I needed that." She wiped her eyes. "Thanks, Julie, for everything. You worked so hard making things right here, and I haven't been here for you at all."

There was one thing I still had to do. It seemed like a good moment. "Mum," I said. "I have to tell you something." I couldn't quite look her in the eye. "I . . . I kind of got Rudy some dog food today." She stiffened.

I hurried on. "I mean, I know you said you wouldn't pay for any food, but he really didn't have any and he was hungry and . . . I'll pay you back, I'll do jobs around the house, I'll mow the lawn . . ."

Mum put her hand up for me to stop. She looked as if she was thinking about everything, really hard. She looked at me, she looked at Rudy, and then back at me.

She smiled, and I felt the breath whoosh out of me. I realised I'd been holding it in for quite a while.

"Julie," she said, "you keep buying food for that crazy dog of yours."

You know, I don't think I'd ever loved my mum as much as I did right then.

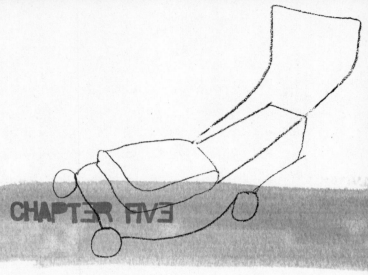

CHAPTER FIVE

When I got up the next morning, Mum had left a note on the table again. She wrote that she hoped I had a good day and that she would bring dinner home tonight and what did I want? I was supposed to call her at the bank and let her know if I wanted Indian, Chinese or pizza, or whatever. I phoned and left a message on her voicemail saying I wanted Chinese.

I tried phoning my dad again, but there was still no answer. It kind of made me mad, you know? Why did it always have to be me trying to get hold of him? I knew my dad loved me. I knew he'd call me when he could and that he gets really busy at work. But still I wished he would ring.

I started to phone Megan. I even picked up the phone and dialled her number, but when her mum answered I suddenly remembered we weren't talking and hung up. I don't know why I forgot. I just did. She probably wouldn't have been home anyway.

She was the one person I talked to about everything. I didn't really have anyone else to talk to. But I still had Rudy.

I gave him some dog biscuits (which he gulped like it was his last meal) and made myself some toast with cinnamon and sugar on it. It tasted really, really good. Rudy watched me eating it and licked his lips. What a pig.

I made another piece, drank a glass of milk and watched TV for a while, but it was pretty boring, so Rudy and I went out in the backyard. What did it matter if I was still in my pyjamas? We sat on the back step and just hung out, you know?

I closed my eyes and leaned back against the house. There was a sweet smell in the air like fresh hay. It smelled so clean. The birds were singing and there was one that made this *whoo-ee-hooo* sound.

I scratched Rudy's head and listened to *whoo-ee-hooo*, over and over. The sun was already warm and I felt very peaceful, you know? As if, somehow, everything would be okay.

Someone started up a lawnmower. It was so loud I couldn't hear the birds singing any more. But the sun was getting pretty hot and the moment had kind of gone anyway. I got the idea that maybe I could cut our lawn – it was looking really bad. I might not have cut the lawn before, but I was pretty sure I could handle it.

"Come on, Rudy, let's go inside," I said. I turned to step through the sliding door and of course he had to go through at the exact same time. We both got jammed for a second. "Geez, Rudy," I said, and we struggled for another second, until he squeezed in ahead of me. Inside, he danced around, panting and smiling, as if he'd done some great trick.

I shook my head at him. "You need to learn some manners, Rudy," I said. But he knew I wasn't really mad.

I got out some work clothes – the sort of thing Dad wore when he worked in the garden – tied my hair back in a ponytail and put on a baseball cap.

We went out to the garage where Dad kept his mower and I rolled it out onto the driveway. Rudy sniffed it and raised his leg, but I yelled at him and he slunk off, sauntered over to one of Mum's rose bushes and peed on that. I yelled at him again, but he was far enough away that he really didn't care.

"Just don't do that in front of Mum," I told him and he grinned at me. I swear he winked, too. "Crazy dog," I muttered.

I turned back to the mower. There were knobs and pull-cords and no instructions on how to get the thing to work. "This could be harder than I thought, Rudy," I said. He came and stood by me as if he was trying to help me figure it out.

"Need some help?" someone called. Our next-door neighbour was hanging over the low fence, wiping his head with a rag. He was an older man whose wife had died last year. I'd never spoken to him much, just "Hi" and "Good morning" and stuff like that.

"Uh . . . yeah. I guess," I said. "Thanks."

"No problem, little lady," he said, like someone out of a cowboy movie or something. He came down his driveway and up ours and opened up the petrol cap to look in. "That's fine," he said. Then he looked in another compartment, for oil, I think, and said that was fine, too. He pressed a button on the motor a couple of times. "This primes it," he said, gripping a lever on the handle. "Now hold down the throttle *while* you pull the cord."

He pulled on the cord and the engine caught and started up. "Real easy if you know how to do it," he shouted over the noise, winking at me. "Not so easy if you don't." He shut it off. "Now you try it."

I just wanted to get started. I wasn't looking for

mowing lessons from some old guy I didn't even know, but he was trying to help and, besides, he'd shut it off. I had to get it started again. I kind of smiled at him, like gee-I-don't-mind-at-all, and bent down to press the button.

"Pump it two or three times," he said. I pumped the button and pulled back on the cord. The engine barely rattled. A sweat broke out on my forehead.

"No, no, you forgot to hold down the throttle. The throttle is like holding down the accelerator in a car. So hold it like this," he said. He clamped my hand on the lever. "Now try it again."

This guy was beginning to get on my nerves. I gripped the throttle, took a deep breath and yanked on the cord, just to shut him up. The engine snarled into life.

I jumped back.

"Holy . . ." I said, with a big, dumb grin on my face. I know it sounds stupid, but I was so proud I'd started it – as if I'd discovered a cure for cancer or something. "Thanks," I shouted.

"Now you know how to start a lawnmower all by yourself," he shouted back.

I nodded. "Yeah, thanks, Mr . . ."

"Name's Ray." He shielded his eyes from the sun. "You have any problems, don't be shy about asking for help. Understand?" I nodded. "Good girl. You take care now, Julie."

He turned and walked back to his garden. And somehow I just knew that he'd seen that whole thing with my parents. And probably all the fights before that, too.

Mowing the lawn is hard work. It's not so much pushing the mower around – that's nothing. It's making sure you don't miss any bits, so your lawn doesn't look as if it's had a bad haircut. I had to crisscross around quite a bit, but I thought it looked pretty good for a first try.

When I'd rolled the lawnmower back into the garage, I noticed that Mum's flowers looked dry, so I uncoiled the hose and turned the tap on all the way. I guess it was too much, because the hose kind of erupted with water, flopping around like a possessed snake.

Rudy lunged at it, grabbing it in his teeth and shaking it (he probably thought he was protecting me) until it sprang about a million holes.

"Oh great!" I shouted. "Just great, you big, dumb dog." I grabbed the hose and blasted him with water while he gulped and snapped at the spray like he was having an attack or something. He looked so stupid, I laughed until my sides hurt.

I was dancing back and forth, too, and I guess it must have been pretty slippery, because I slipped and landed on my back. Rudy pounced on me and slobbered all over my face, which is pretty gross, I guess, but I was laughing so hard I didn't care.

As we were rolling around on the wet grass, I noticed Brianna, Suze and Jessica walking by.

"Stop it, Rudy," I shouted, pushing him away and sitting up. "Hey," I called.

The three of them stopped. "Hi, Julie," said Jessica.

"Hi," said Brianna. Suze was looking away, as if there was something very, very interesting in the distance. I tried to get up, but Rudy bowled me over again, furiously wagging his tail and rump. "That's enough!" I said, pushing him off. His ears went back and he slunk to the ground.

I finally got up, pulled my wet clothes into some sort of order and got my hair out of my eyes. "So what are you guys up to?" I asked. Suze kept studying whatever it was she found so fascinating, but she didn't say anything.

"Just hanging around," muttered Jessica. Brianna

shrugged halfheartedly.

Suddenly I felt as if I had the plague.

"Is something wrong?" I asked.

Suze smiled this prissy smile that made me want to slap her. She still wouldn't look at me. Brianna stared at the ground. "See you, Julie," she said.

Three girls walk away, down the long street, leaving just one, a leafless tree, alone. Everything tilts. The ocean, the tree . . . The dog holds me rooted to the ground with his soft, brown eyes.

I curled up on the couch. I had changed back into my pyjamas, even though the sun was still up. Rudy jumped up and settled in where my legs were bent. He fell asleep right away, but I couldn't sleep, even though I was tired.

I kept thinking about things, thoughts buzzing in my head until I almost felt dizzy. I don't even know what I was thinking about. There was this hollow space inside me, as if someone had carved out a piece.

I don't know how long I lay there, just thinking about stuff. Rudy was snoring quietly when the phone rang. I shook him off and he slunk away down the hall as I ran to answer it.

"Hello?" I said.

"Baby! Finally I've got you on the phone."

"Dad! I . . ."

"Listen, babe, I don't have time to talk right now, but how about I swing by on Saturday and pick you up for the weekend. What do you say?"

"I'd love that!"

"And don't worry about Evie, baby. She wants to meet you. So don't worry about it."

"Oh . . . yeah." I had forgotten about Evie. "Are you sure it's okay?"

"Sure I am, baby, but leave that dog of yours at home."

"Dad," I said. "I *can't* leave Rudy here. Mum would never agree to that."

There was a silence and my gut kind of tightened. "Dad, please. I really want to see you. I haven't seen you since . . . well, you know."

There were a few more seconds of silence, then he swore softly to himself. "Yeah, bring it then," he said with a sigh. "I'll say something to Evie. I love you, babe."

"I love you, too, Da . . ."

The phone went dead.

I phoned him right back, because I didn't even know what time he was coming or anything. There was no answer, but it didn't matter at all, because he had rung and I was finally going to see him again!

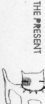

"Rudy, guess what?" I called. "Guess what . . . Hey, where are you?" I heard a thump (he must have jumped off my bed) and he came running out into the hall, wagging his tail like he was trying to take off. "We finally get to see Dad . . . We finally get to see Dad!" I sang.

I grabbed his front paws and we were dancing around the living room when my mum asked, "What's the occasion?" She was standing in the front doorway, holding a big takeaway bag, a greasy stain leaching up one side.

I dropped Rudy's paws. I suddenly felt guilty, you know, as if I'd been caught stealing or something. "Um, Dad just rang and he's picking me up on Saturday."

It was as if my mum's eyes were suddenly carved out of stone. Her jaw got hard, and her mouth was working like she was chewing something bitter.

"Your father should have asked me first if it was okay," she said, spitting out the words. "I had plans for us to go to the movies and spend some time together." She kept staring at me. I didn't know what she wanted from me. "But if you really want to go . . . then go."

"I do," I said. "I really do. But," I added quickly, "I also really want to spend time with you. I just haven't seen him for so long, you know?" Mum nodded without saying anything.

"Maybe we can go out during the week, or something, or maybe next weekend?"

My mum nodded again. She put the bag of food on the table.

The day is so clear, I feel as if I can jump off the mountain and fly. The mountain range gathers around me – beautiful, white-robed, pristine . . .

The ocean looms far below me. I know it is there, but I do not look down. I will not look down. But my feet slip and I fall . . .

I try to scream, but my voice sticks in my throat. I fall headfirst towards the ink that swirls like a thick whirlpool, towards its dark, gurgling centre . . . and still I cannot scream . . .

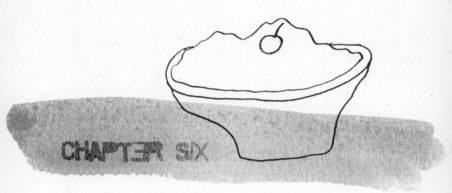

"Well, that's it," I said. Rudy stood with his nose in my suitcase, snuffling.

My bag was packed: toothbrush and toothpaste, hairbrush, five pairs of underwear, five pairs of socks, two pairs of jeans (I was wearing the third pair) and four shirts, not including the one I had on. I thought about bringing a book or something, just in case they didn't have a TV. I threw one in.

Rudy (who was still snuffling) gave a gigantic, wet snort, like he'd inhaled pepper or something, and stared at me.

I looked back at him for a second before it dawned on me. "Oh yeah!" I said and ran into the kitchen, Rudy scrambling after me on the tile floor. I got his dog food and grabbed his leash. "Can't forget about you, right, boy?" Rudy panted and wagged his tail, his eyes forming half-moons.

I made my bed, did the dishes and put them away. I wiped the table (I wanted to make sure I didn't leave any mess for Mum to have to clean up when she got home) and I even vacuumed the living room, making sure all the strokes on the carpet went in one direction, the way Mum liked it.

It was 10.30, Saturday morning. Mum had gone before I got up. She left a note saying to phone if I wanted to and that she loved me. It was nice.

I tried ringing Dad to see what time he was coming, but there was no answer.

I wanted to talk to Megan so badly. I couldn't even remember why we'd fought. Because Rudy threw up? It seemed like a dumb reason to stay mad, so I picked up the phone and dialled her number.

"Hello," she said.

"Megan? It's Julie."

"Hi."

"Umm . . . Megan, I just wanted to say sorry again for everything the other day. I . . . hope you got the vomit out of everything."

There was silence. Then Megan sighed and said, "That's okay, Jules. Sorry I went off at you like that. But you know Kevin has been going through some hard times and you kind of hurt my feelings."

What about my hard times, I wanted to say, but I

didn't. "Yeah . . . I'm really sorry."

"Maybe you can come over later," she said.

"Oh, I can't. My dad's coming to get me for the weekend. But I can come over when I get back, okay?"

"Okay. Bye."

"Bye."

I hung up.

I guess I felt better, but I also felt sad. It was crazy, I know. I just felt as if Megan was a stranger sometimes, even though I've known her since forever.

It was 10.45. Only fifteen minutes had passed. I tried ringing Dad again. No answer.

I can't remember what I did all morning and afternoon. I think I worked on more tricks with Rudy (I would show Dad the "Bang" one, too) and he did okay. I was so desperate I watched a soap opera.

Finally – it was maybe 4.30 or something – I heard Dad's truck. I shrieked, scaring Rudy because he jumped off the couch and I swear his fur stood on end, and ran to the window. Dad's truck was outside and he was honking the horn.

"Come on, babe!" he shouted out the window.

I ran across the grass with my suitcase, like in

a slow-motion movie. I could see his smile, see his face, hear his voice . . .

I was halfway into the truck when I noticed Rudy had stopped in the middle of the lawn. "Rudy," I called. He didn't move. *"Rudy!"*

He walked slowly to the truck, skirting around the front to where I was standing with the door open. "What's wrong with you?" I asked him. "Get in!"

"Crazy mutt!" said Dad, as Rudy scrambled into the back and I settled down with my suitcase balanced on my lap. Dad leaned over and grabbed me in his arms. "Baby, it's so good to see you. I missed you."

You know, I couldn't say a thing, my throat felt so tight. I was so happy.

He stroked my hair and I guess I started to cry. I didn't mean to, it just kind of happened. I cried so hard that snot hung down off my nose in a string and my eyes felt hot and swollen.

"I'm sorry," I said and I did a lame attempt at a laugh (my nose was so clogged, I blew out a snot bubble).

"Hey, don't be stupid. It's okay," he said, laughing. He wiped my cheek with his sleeve, took my chin in his hand and looked me in the eyes. "Everything's okay now. I'm here."

Then he put his truck into gear and we roared off. It was one of the happiest moments of my life.

Ten minutes later we pulled into the driveway of a small, white house. It was surrounded by tall pines, with a few green shrubs shaped like puffballs. A basket of blood-red flowers hung outside the front door. The nearest neighbour was a minute down the street.

I stood in the doorway, Rudy beside me, holding my suitcase.

"Evie?" Dad called. He stood there, waiting and listening.

"Just a minute," called a voice. A door opened and a woman as short as me came out. Only she was way prettier. Her auburn hair was curled and styled like a shampoo model and her eyes were a beautiful green moss colour (it doesn't sound pretty, but it was, believe me). She reminded me of a tiny, perfect cat.

She held out a delicate, white hand. I grasped it in my paw and I think babbled my name. With golf-ball swollen eyes and dried snot all over my face, I'm sure I looked fabulous, you know? Only she smiled as if I was the sweetest thing since bees invented honey.

"You must be Julie." She smiled even wider, showing small, perfect (of course), pearly-white teeth. Now she bent down to Rudy. "And who are you?" She patted his head.

Rudy snarled and curled up his lip.

"Rudy!" I said. I smacked his nose and he yelped.

Evie pulled back. A look flashed in her eyes and was quickly gone. I couldn't even swear I'd seen it, but I felt a stab of fear in the pit of my stomach.

She smiled at me, shaking her head. "Dogs are so unpredictable, aren't they?"

At dinner the three of us ate together. Evie chewed her food in this round, circular way, kind of like the way a cow chews its cud, but somehow she made it look good. She kept looking at my father and smiling, with her head kind of tilted to one side.

Rudy had been banished to the far corner, where he sat staring at Evie.

We were having pork chops with potatoes and

some sort of green vegetable.

"This is delicious," I said to Evie, just to be polite, because actually I was having trouble chewing the pork. It was really tough.

"Thank you, Julie." She took another pork chop from the platter and put it on my plate. "Have another." She smiled at me with her white teeth.

"Yeah, Julie likes her food. Don't you, babe?" Dad elbowed me in the ribs and Evie laughed her high, tinkling laugh. I looked at him and he smiled fondly back. He really hadn't a clue that he'd said anything wrong. He looked like a kid at Christmas, with Evie on one side and the-daughter-who-likes-her-food on the other.

Evie watched and smiled, looking like a saint in a cathedral as I ate each bite.

I don't know how, but I managed to choke down that stupid pork chop.

"I have a surprise for dessert," she said. She got up from the table and at that exact moment I noticed that Rudy wasn't in his corner any more.

Evie called from the kitchen. "I made this just for . . ." There was a crash. *"YOU IDIOT DOG, YOU . . ."*

Rudy came hurtling out of the kitchen with what looked like whipped cream all over his face. Either that or he had rabies.

Then Evie followed, holding a large bowl. Spatters of cream and red gooey stuff were smeared down the sides.

"I . . . I'm so sorry," I said.

Dad stared at the bowl, wide-eyed.

Evie took a deep breath and smiled her tight, pearly smile. Shaking her head in a what-can-you-do-with-that-stupid-dog kind of way, she turned to my dad. "It seems Julie's dog has eaten our dessert." The tinkling laugh sounded again. "You're out of luck, partner!"

My dad looked at her and then at Rudy, who was licking cream off his lips, and burst out laughing. "Man, oh man! That dog is something else!" He slapped his knee and looked at Rudy.

But Evie was looking straight at me.

"I'll go out and get something. Don't worry, Evie." Dad was still laughing as he grabbed his keys and made for the door.

"Dad, wait!" I called, but the door had slammed behind him.

Evie walked towards me, her eyes never leaving my face. She stood in front of me. "You think you're funny?" she asked. A little smile played on her lips. Her green eyes bored into me.

"Umm, no. I didn't know Rudy was . . ."

"You know what? You are a stupid little girl." Evie leaned in so close I could smell her perfume. She reached up her hand, on which each long nail was painted a perfect, glossy red, and tucked a wisp of hair behind my ear. My heart hammered in my chest.

Rudy growled at her from the corner.

Just then my dad walked back in. "Forgot my wallet," he said. He stopped, seeing the two of us. "Uh, everything okay?"

Evie smiled. "Perfect," she said. "I was fixing Julie's hair."

I tried to speak, you know, I really did try, but my voice wouldn't come out. I looked at my dad. My eyes screamed, *Don't leave me, don't leave me . . .*

"You go, Charlie. We'll be fine." Evie smiled at me. "We'll have some girl time. Right, Julie?" She winked at me.

No . . .

Dad had already turned back to the door.

"Oh and, Charlie honey?" she said. "Take that dog with you."

I heard the truck leave. Evie moved behind me, silent. The hairs on my neck stood straight up, but I couldn't move.

"Julie," she whispered in my ear, "this is *my* house." Something crashed behind me. Slivers of glass skittered across the floor. I jumped.

"That was my favourite," said Evie. She sounded disgusted. "My grandmother gave it to me. Irreplaceable!"

Something flew by my ear, shattering against the wall in front of me. "That was worth six hundred dollars!" she said.

I shook my head. Please . . .

Now she walked around to stand in front of me.

She laughed softly. "You won't know what hit you, little girl."

I watch from the ceiling. I feel concern for the girl. Glad it's not me.

Why does the girl just stand there? Rooted to the spot. Why can't she open her mouth? Say something? Say anything?

"What the . . ." said my dad, opening the door. Broken glass crunched against the door and under his feet.

"EVIE," he cried, going to the woman huddled against the wall, weeping.

THE PRESENT

Rudy stood in the doorway, whining. The broken glass circled me like a ring of thorns.

"Evie, baby, tell me what happened."

She whimpered, clutching at his shirt and burying her face in his chest, pointing a shaking, perfect, clawed finger at me. "She . . . she's crazy!"

I ride in the truck. The ocean beats in my head. . .

"Tell me why you did it . . . Just tell me why you did it," he screams, punching a fist on the steering wheel. Drops of spit fly from his mouth. One lands on my hand. I say nothing. I watch the bubble of spit slowly dry from the edges, towards its centre.

Rudy whines gently behind me.

CHAPTER SEVEN

You'd think I'd run home, crying to Mum, but I didn't. I didn't tell anybody what happened. I just couldn't bring myself to, you know? Like I had something to be ashamed of. Part of me thought, what would make a grown-up woman do something like that? I must have asked for it somehow.

And then right after that another part of me said, *Don't be stupid*. That's all. *Don't be stupid*.

I got out my bike on Sunday morning and rode to the cemetery with Rudy in tow. I didn't call Megan. I didn't try to ring my dad. Mum was still in her room, so I didn't wake her up. I wanted to be alone and have time to think about things.

As I cycled along, Rudy ran beside me. You know, he really is a smart dog, because he didn't swerve in front like last time. He ran right next to me. He learns fast when he wants to.

I thought about everything Evie had done. How she'd said I'd broken her stuff – as if one minute I could be perfectly normal and the next minute go completely insane and toss glass ornaments around. I mean, does that make any sense to you? Because it doesn't to me. I have never thrown things (well, maybe when I was, like, two or something). And my dad doesn't even know me well enough to get that his girlfriend is lying. He believed *her*?

That really, really hurt my feelings. And it made me mad. Why hadn't I said something?

I pedalled so hard – I guess because I was angry – that Rudy was foaming at the mouth, so I slowed down a little. Poor guy!

We got to the old graveyard and it was like walking into a bubble. No traffic noise, only birds singing, a smell of sweet hay in the air . . . a good place to think.

I found a spot on the hill that wasn't too near a grave and lay down spread-eagled on the grass. Rudy settled next to me, his panting slowing, until he lowered his head and flopped on his side.

I just breathed for a while and watched clouds shift in the sky.

I felt like a small dot on the side of a huge ball, as if I was connected to the universe. I know it sounds stupid, but sometimes I think that, when things are really, really bad, you find something inside that you didn't know was there before. Something good. Maybe it takes something horrible to wake it up, you know?

I can't really explain it, but it just seemed like at that moment I understood everything. I understood how my parents had screwed up and that none of this was my fault. I understood that right now my life really stank, but deep, deep inside I knew I was meant for something better than this.

After a while we got up and wandered around the tombstones. I've always liked imagining what people were like who lived a long time ago, so when we were walking around I made up stories about people buried there.

"Well, you know, Rudy," I said, "when young *Thomas Alistair McCready* was in his prime, he sailed the seven seas and brought spices back from . . ." I looked at Rudy, who was listening intently. "Where *do* spices come from?" I asked. Rudy tilted his head at me like, duh . . . I dunno.

"Umm . . . Okay, young Thomas brought back

treasure and an untold fortune and buried it. And to this day there are those who believe that the treasure lies buried with young Tom himself . . ." And so on. I really started getting into it.

"And then there was the notorious *Willard Ebenezer Morrison*, a womanising scoundrel and ne'er-do-well." We strolled to another marker. "And here," I waved my arm towards the stone like a tour guide, "lies the sickly yet devastatingly handsome *Isaac Baldwin Jackson*." Rudy sniffed the stone and peed on it. "Geez, Rudy," I said. "Show some respect."

I rested my hand on top of another gravestone. "And, of course, we must not forget the stalwart *Frances Price O'Neill*, upon whose back the nations of the free world stand." I had no idea what all that actually meant, but it sounded good, and Rudy seemed to like it.

We came to Elizabeth's grave. Tall, weedy grass gathered around the headstone, leaning in the breeze that swept up the hill, making the leaves of the tree overhead shift and shimmer.

I sat down and stared at the grave. Rudy looked at me expectantly. "You want to hear about Elizabeth?" He winked at me, so I took that as a yes.

It had to be special for little Elizabeth, so I

thought for a minute. "Baby Elizabeth was born a healthy, chubby-cheeked cherub and by rights should have had a life of utter, unending joy. But her parents, though honest folk, were poor and couldn't spend money on frivolities like new shoes and a proper coat and hat. And so it was that, in the chilly November of 1956, little Elizabeth caught a cold. 'It will go away,' said her mother. 'She's as strong as an ox,' said her father. But, alas, it was not so. Poor Elizabeth died of her cold and it was only then, as her mother and father turned their tear-filled eyes towards the cruel heavens, that they realised what a gift their precious child had been, now to be an angel forever more."

And you know what? I started to choke myself up. Rudy put his head on my knee as I sobbed out baby Elizabeth's concocted story. I was in full swing when a voice behind me asked, "Uh . . . are you okay?"

I screamed like the star in a slasher movie and whipped around. Rudy scrambled to his feet, woofing and snarling, but not really being convincing, because he looked kind of scared, too.

A guy, probably a little older than me, stood staring like I'd sprouted five heads. His hands were up in front of him as if to say *I-come-in-peace*. For someone who had heard me crying and gabbling to myself, he didn't look too freaked out.

"Oh," I said, wiping a smear of snot across my cheek. "I was just ..." I didn't even finish. It sounded too lame.

"How d'you know all that stuff?" he asked.

I could lie. I could say I was a junior historian or Elizabeth was my great-great-grandmother (except that she died when she was two), but instead I said, "I made it up."

"Okaaaay," he said. He stared at me with a look like, should I run now or later? But then he shrugged. "That's cool. Doesn't matter to me. Name's Jordan." He stuck out his hand and then quickly pulled it back when he saw my slime-encrusted hand.

"Yeah, sorry," I said, wiping it on the grass. "I'm Julie and this ferocious beast is Rudy." Rudy panted at him, smiling.

Jordan bent down and let his hand be sniffed by Rudy, who then allowed Jordan to scratch him behind the ears. "Anyway, what are you doing here in a graveyard, crying like that?"

"I don't know." Usually I'd feel kind of embarrassed talking about stuff like that with a stranger, so I didn't say anything else for a second, but Jordan looked at me as he scratched Rudy's ears, waiting, as if he really wanted to hear the answer.

I shrugged. "I guess it's been a pretty tough summer. My dad left my mum and me a couple of weeks ago."

Jordan shook his head. "Man, that *is* rough. My sister's husband left her and her kid and she's living at home again in our basement. My mum and dad help her out, but still . . ." He let the sentence hang in the air, then smiled at me before squinting into the sun. "I usually help take care of my nephew, but today I didn't have to."

He sat down next to me, then scratched out a pebble from the dirt and lobbed it lazily into the air. It landed near the bottom of the hill, rolling to a stop.

"Where do you live?" I asked.

He pointed in the same direction Megan lived in. "Down the hill, right through those trees. First brick house." He hesitated for a moment. "I come up here a lot because . . ." he said, shrugging. "I don't know. I like it. It's peaceful."

I nodded. "Yeah. I like it, too." We looked out over the hill, not saying anything for a while. But it wasn't a silence where you want to start giggling because you feel so stupid. It was comfortable, you know? I could see the snake of road skirting along the bottom of the hill, but up there I felt higher than the clouds.

The sun was getting low over the horizon. "I've got to go," I said. "I live over that way," and pointed towards town.

"Maybe I'll see you around, Julie," said Jordan. "See you, Rudy. You're a good dog." He stroked Rudy's head and Rudy licked his hand.

"Yeah," I said. "See you around."

Halfway down, he waved, but kept on walking.

CHAPTER EIGHT

Mum was lying on the couch when I got home. I said hello, and she rolled over, smiling.

"Julie," she said and held out her arms to me.

When I leaned over to hug her, her breath smelled funny and I kind of wanted to get away, but I didn't say anything. I didn't want to hurt her feelings. I held my breath and after a minute or so I stood up and breathed again.

"Uh . . . Mum, you said you wanted to go to the movies. Do you still want to? There's a . . ."

"No," she whispered. "No." She waved her hand in front of her face like she was batting away a pesky fly.

I stared at her for a minute. "Are you okay?"

She snorted. "Am I okay? Am I?" She looked at me, then she flipped herself around so she faced the couch and not me. "I'm fine," she muttered.

She'd been drinking. I gritted my teeth against the tears that filled my eyes. I had thought I was pretty strong after what happened with my dad and Evie, but I couldn't take any more. I totally lost it.

I started yelling at her. "Who do you think you are, leaving me alone like this? Dad left me, too! I'm going through this, too! Not just you!" And you know the big response I got? Nothing.

I felt like shaking her until she dealt with her problems, instead of running away and leaving me here alone.

My heart felt as if it was going to burst in my chest and I was breathing really fast. I took Rudy and went out for a walk to keep myself from exploding into a million pieces.

The stars were out. How could the stars be out, twinkling? How could the moon be up in the sky like everything was so normal when it was all just one big lie?

I sat down on the curb and rocked back and forth, shaking my head, trying to get away from myself.

Rudy leaned against me, his head on my knee, looking up at me with sad, brown eyes. "You're my only friend," I said, and hugged him so hard he began to whimper and wriggle.

Eventually, I had to go home. There was nowhere

else to go. Mum was still draped across the couch.

I crept into the kitchen, got the phone and took Rudy with me to my room, jamming a chair under the door handle.

I flopped on my bed and rang Megan.

"Hi, Julie. Isn't it kind of late?"

I didn't even know what time it was. I looked at my alarm clock. 11.15. "Sorry . . . I just really need to talk to someone." And then I got choked up. I couldn't even get a word out, you know?

"Jules, what's wrong?" She must have asked me a dozen times.

Finally I managed to speak. "My mum is lying on the couch doing nothing, and I was supposed to go to my dad's this weekend, but his girlfriend . . ." I couldn't talk again.

Megan was silent for a moment. She said, "I'm really sorry, Jules. It's so weird that you had problems, too, because actually Kevin had this problem with *his* mum this weekend and he's . . ."

For a second I stared at the phone. I just couldn't believe it. "Megan," I said, almost shouting. "I don't care what happened to Kevin, okay? This is happening to *me*!" Megan started to say something, but I cut her off. "You act like you don't even care! All you talk about is Kevin. Well, I've got my own problems to worry about and I'm sick of nobody caring about what . . . "

There was a click and the line went dead. She hung up on me? I screamed into the phone, "I never liked Kevin anyway!" and threw it at the wall.

I lie curled on my bed and the room swirls around me, a carousel of ink-black shadows. I am lost in a dark room without a door . . .

———

The weak morning light peered through my blinds. I had no idea how long I'd slept. Rudy was pawing at the door, needing to get out for a pee.

I groaned and he scratched again and whined. "Okay, okay. I'm coming." I hoisted myself off the bed. My head felt like it was a metre wide and every bit of it throbbed.

Out in the living room, Mum was still lying on the couch. It was Monday morning and she was still here. I looked at the clock on the stove. 10.45am.

"Mum. Get up!"

She rolled over and grunted.

"Mum, get up! You're late for work!" I pulled on her arm. Behind me, Rudy peed on the living room carpet. I'd forgotten all about him.

"RUDY!" He couldn't stop, his legs quivering as he emptied himself. (And apparently there was a lot to empty.)

"Mum! GET UP!" I yelled, running for paper towels. Rudy ran after me, snapping at my heels and barking – he must have thought I was playing a game or something.

I stopped in the kitchen (Rudy skidded into the back of my leg) and tried to catch my breath. I was biting my lip to keep from screaming my head off, like the only sane person in the crazy ward.

I looked at Rudy, panting and smiling. He hadn't a clue.

I was blotting up the pee when Mum sat up and sniffed. "What's that terrible smell?"

"Don't worry about it, Mum," I snapped at her. "You're late for work." I mean, I know she's my mum, but I'd had it, you know?

Her bleary eyes grew wide. "I . . . I'm late?" She looked around blinking.

"It's 10.45. No wait, 10.53 now."

"Oh . . . oh no . . ." She tried to get off the couch, but her leg was trapped by a blanket, so I went over and ripped it off.

"I . . . I have to . . . I . . . I need to . . ." She got off the couch and ran one way, stopped, turned and ran the other. I would have laughed, but it really wasn't funny. Especially when she stepped in Rudy's pee.

"AAAAAaaaaaaaggh!" She held up her foot and stared at it, like it had been dipped in acid. "Wha . . .?"

"It's nothing, Mum. Go have a shower, okay? Here's a towel." It was like she was eight years old and I was the mum.

When I heard the shower running, I rang Mum's work. "This is Julie Walker, Claire's daughter. I wanted to let you know that my mum woke up feeling ill this morning. But she's feeling much better now and she told me to tell you she's on her way." Whoever took the message told me thank you for calling, dear.

I banged on the bathroom door. "Come on, get out. You've got to go."

She came out dripping, wrapped in a towel, looking only slightly more clear-eyed. "Coffee," she muttered.

"I'll get it," I said. "You get dressed." I put in an extra scoop of coffee, just to make sure it was strong enough. When the coffee was done, I poured the whole pot, black, into a giant travel mug, and carried it with both hands into Mum's room. Surprisingly, she had managed to get dressed and sort of dry her hair. It was dry enough, anyway.

She was putting in earrings. She actually looked like Mum again.

"Wow!" she said, taking the mug from me. "That's a lot of coffee. Thanks, Julie. What would I do without you?"

I managed a tight-lipped smile, but I didn't say anything. That could wait.

I stared at her pretty coldly. I could see I was hurting her feelings, but I didn't care, if you want to know the truth. She ducked her head, closed her eyes and nodded.

When Mum was nearly out the door, she turned to me. "I'm sorry," she said. Her eyes looked so sad. She tried to hug me, but I didn't hug her back. I felt like a wooden soldier, my arms glued to my sides.

She tried to smile and said, "I love you, Julie." I watched from behind the living room curtains as she got into her car. She sat for a moment, wiping tears from her cheeks, before driving away.

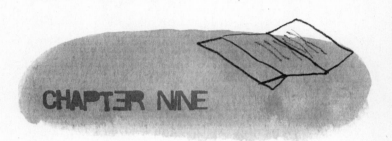

CHAPTER NINE

In one way, I felt like a cold-hearted you-know-what, treating my own mum that way. But in another way I didn't feel bad at all. I thought it was time the adults started *acting* like adults, not me. I was the *kid*, you know? Okay, I was fourteen and pretty mature for my age, but still.

And as far as Megan was concerned, I didn't care if I never talked to her again. I mean, I phone her in the middle of the night, in the middle of a *crisis*, and she starts talking about *Kevin*? I wasn't even sure who she was any more, and maybe I didn't care anyway.

I think Rudy wanted to go for a walk because he kept staring at me, but I was too mad. I paced back and forth in the living room while he watched me. He looked like he was watching a tennis match, but it didn't make me laugh. It just annoyed me.

"Rudy, go and lie down or something!" He didn't move. "Rudy!" I stomped my foot in his direction. He slunk away and disappeared into my room.

I decided I was going to talk to Mum and Dad. I'd talk to Mum tonight. Today, I'd write Dad a letter.

Dad had taken his computer, so I ripped some lined paper from one of my old school notebooks, sat at the kitchen table and wrote.

Dad,

I need to write to you and tell you about what really happened at Evie's. She was the one who broke everything, <u>not</u> <u>me</u>.

I swear that when you left she just started throwing things and going kind of crazy.

I don't know why she did it, but she said something like, "You're in <u>my</u> house now, stupid girl." I can't remember exactly.

I actually feel really mad that you thought I could do that. I mean, I'm your daughter. If you don't know me by now, then I must be a terrible daughter or something.

I don't even know what to say to you.

Julie
P.S. I still love you, but I don't know if you still love

me. I hope you at least believe me because I'm telling the truth.

I would deliver it to his work that day. He's always on a job site (he's a construction foreman), but I could deliver it to the office. They would make sure he got it.

Rudy and I started out. I thought I was pretty sure of the way, but things look different when you're riding a bike, instead of sitting in a car. And then you realise, oh yeah, this is such-and-such a place.

Anyway, I got turned around and by the time we finally got there I swear it was almost going-home time. I tied Rudy's leash to a lamp post outside (he started yowling immediately) then gave the letter to the lady behind the reception desk. She promised me Dad would get it first thing in the morning, and what was that awful noise?

By the time I rescued Rudy, he was foaming again and I was really hungry. I hadn't brought any money, so I couldn't afford to get lost on the way back.

I was staring at the street signs for a minute when a young girl of around six or seven walked by with her mum and dad. She kind of reminded me of myself at that age. She was in between them, holding each of their hands and looking up at them with a look on her face like you-two-are-the-best-parents-ever. She was skipping and singing and I could tell she really thought it would be like that forever.

I would have given anything to be that little girl for just one second.

I didn't get too lost on the way home, so we were back before dark, which was lucky. I wasn't ready to face Mum yet, so Rudy and I sat on the front step. I scratched behind his ears and he nestled his head into my lap and got pretty comfortable.

I hadn't been paying much attention to him. I'd been mad all day, and mad at him, too, even though he hadn't done anything. I felt kind of guilty about that so, when he started to drool on my leg, I didn't even make him move his head.

The sun was setting and the street lights were just flickering on when Mum opened the door. "Julie," she said.

I didn't turn around.

"Julie, can we talk?" I ignored her. "Julie! Answer

me! No matter what's happened, I'm still your mother, so answer me when I . . ."

"Then act like it!" I shouted, flinging myself around to face her and knocking Rudy off my lap. "If you're still my mum, why don't you . . ." I burst out crying so hard, the tears flung out into the air like confetti. I'd never spoken to my mum like that before.

"Julie . . ." I felt her arms around me and I didn't move for a second. Then my arms flew around her and we just kind of clung to each other.

"Julie," she said, "forgive me."

Of course. Yes.

The next morning I felt filled with light, you know what I mean? Like after a terrible storm and the next day the sun is out and you can't get over how beautiful it all is. My mum made it to work and I felt like I could breathe for the first time in a week. I had delivered the letter to my dad, so he would understand and I felt good about that, too. Maybe things were going to be okay after all. They couldn't have got much worse.

I played with Rudy in the backyard and then we

both went for a swim. Rudy had been chasing me around the garden, snapping at my heels. When he does that, I can't help but scream, you know? Maybe a caveman part of my brain remembers being chased, even though I know Rudy wouldn't hurt me. Anyway, I jumped into the pool to escape and he, of course, dived in right on top of me.

"Geez, Rudy," I spluttered, "you're going to drown me!" He didn't seem too concerned, paddling around me in circles with this big grin on his face and his fur sticking up in spikes on his head. He looked so stupid, I could hardly keep treading water because I was laughing so hard. What a stupid dog!

I winged the Frisbee to the other end of the pool and he lunged ferociously after it.

"Good boy!" I said. "Now bring it here." He ignored me. I dived after him, trying to get the Frisbee, but he kept moving it from one side to the other with his mouth, keeping it just out of my reach.

"I command you to bring it to me!" I said, in what I thought was a stern, authoritarian voice, just like the library video recommended, but he must have thought I said paddle away faster or something, because that's what he did.

I climbed out of the pool and ran around the edge until I reached him. "INCOMING," I shrieked, as he tried frantically to paddle away, and I dropped on him. I had to cling to him like I was barrel riding, but I finally got that Frisbee from his stupid jaws. And when I did I hoisted it in triumph, like it was the Olympics or something. "HA!"

At that moment I saw my dad watching from the gate. Rudy snatched the Frisbee from my hand and swam away. Suddenly I felt cold. I swam to the edge, climbed out and stood there, waiting. I guess Rudy saw I wasn't playing any more, or maybe he knew something was up, because he scrambled out of the pool and came running over to stand by me, dripping.

Dad walked over slowly. He had circles under his eyes and his hair was uncombed. Rudy shook himself right next to him. "Stupid mutt!" said Dad. And then, "Sorry." He sat heavily on a deckchair.

"Got your note," he said. He looked at the ground. "I don't know what to say." He ran his hands through his hair. He looked around and grabbed another deckchair. "Here, baby, sit down." I didn't move. "Please . . ."

I sat down stiffly.

He took my hand and I swear I saw tears in his

eyes. I'd never seen him cry before. "Baby, I know you're angry." I didn't move. "I know it hasn't been easy for you with your mum and me." He rubbed his free hand over his face, shaking his head. "If I could change things, I would. You know that, don't you?"

I sat like a statue, not speaking.

"I . . . I thought I knew how things were, but then, when you acted like that, I could see that this separation was really . . ."

When you acted like that . . . When you acted like that . . . The ocean surges in my head, crashing, spinning. He doesn't believe me . . . He doesn't believe me.

Dad buried his face in his hands. "I just don't know why you did it, baby. If you were hurting that much . . ." He shook his head. "And then writing that letter? I mean, that just made it worse . . ."

"GET OUT!" I scream. "GET OUT!" I lunge at him with my own small claws. He grabs my puny hands, tears shining on his cheeks. He lets go and I fall, like a tumbling leaf, over my dog and land, silently, on my back.

Thick clouds skitter across the blue-jewel sky.

CHAPTER TEN

I sat at Elizabeth's grave, yanking out the weeds that clustered around the headstone. I hadn't played with Rudy. I hadn't spoken to Mum last night. I don't know what she thought. Maybe she thought I was still angry with her. I wouldn't come out of my room for dinner.

"Julie, please," she'd said, but I just stared at the ceiling, not wanting to listen. Rudy scratched at my door. I wouldn't let him in, either.

I left Rudy at home and rode alone to the graveyard. He watched me leave from the living room window, his eyes sad and confused.

There were dark clouds overhead. I didn't care. I lay back and stretched out my arms, running my hands over the grass. What a fool I'd been to think things couldn't get worse. Things could always get worse.

What a fool I'd been to think my dad would believe me.

I couldn't even cry. My heart felt like a stone in my chest. The good things I'd felt were meant for me, the dreams I'd had about being happy – that all seemed so childish.

I held on to the earth and together we turned, under a sky that threatened rain.

I slip off the rock and fall head first into the black, gurgling centre. I hit the water. Ink fills my nostrils, my eyes, my mouth . . .

I struggle and paw at the thick, black water. I try to see which way is up, but I cannot see . . . I cannot see . . .

"JULIE." Someone shakes my shoulder and I hear the sound of sobbing. To my surprise, it is me. Blindly, I take the warm hand touching mine. "It's okay," says the voice. "You're okay."

I open my eyes. Jordan is kneeling beside me, holding my hand in his. "It's okay . . . It's going to be okay."

It had started to rain. "Come on," he said and led me down the hill to my bike. He let go of my hand to pull the bike upright and wheel it across the grass, heading in the opposite direction to my house.

"I'm taking you to my house. My mum would kill me if I left you out in the rain." He smiled, his eyes not leaving mine.

The wet grass slapped against my bare legs and rain trickled down my hair in little rivers. The rain on the soil filled the air with a dusky perfume.

Jordan's house looked snug, tucked in behind a stand of old maples. Through the trees I could just make out the graveyard on the hill.

I suddenly realised I was going to a stranger's house. I mean, I didn't know Jordan at all. Maybe he was an axe murderer or something and had a dozen bodies hidden in the basement.

I looked at him, wheeling my bike through the rain, his hair soggy from standing outside holding my hand. Why should he care about me? For some reason he seemed to.

He propped my bike against the massive maple next to the driveway. Flowers fringed the stones, all different colours – daisies, pansies, tea roses, others I didn't know ... The smell from the flowers and the wet soil made me want to lie down on a big pile of leaves and sleep.

A woman opened the door, and held it open

for us. Her dark hair hung in tight ringlets to her shoulders and she had kind eyes. She reminded me of Megan's mum, with her apple cheeks, only her skin was darker.

"Jordan, who is this?"

"Mum, this is Julie. Julie, this is my mum, Celeste."

She took my hands, held them in hers and looked into my eyes. "Julie, nice to meet you. Come on in and get warmed up. Your hands are ice cold! Jordan, go get her a towel."

Jordan went off to find a towel and Celeste led me into the living room. I met Jordan's sister Sheree and her son Trevor. I'm not great at guessing babies' ages, but I think he looked around ten or eleven months. He was plopped on a colourful mat (you know the kind, with mirrors and squeaky things and painted-on bullseyes) like a big sweet potato. He smiled at me, showing his one gleaming white tooth and a shining gob of drool on his chin.

Jordan's sister sat with Trevor, shaking a rattle. She looked up at me and nodded hello. She looked tired.

The smell of roasting meat filled my nostrils.

"Now, Julie," said Celeste. "You are welcome to stay for dinner. We have plenty."

Dinner at Jordan's house was difficult. I know this sounds weird, but it was because they were so nice – even to each other, you know what I mean? It was like I was starving and they had this feast set out that they had every day. Feasting on ham and turkey and fresh apple pie, while I'm sitting here chewing on an old bone. I mean, that's what my life could've been like if my parents weren't acting like such you-know-whats. It made me so sad.

After dinner, Jordan's dad Gerald put my bike into their van. I sat in the front seat, with Jordan in the back, and he drove me home. I don't know what we talked about though, because I suddenly remembered that I had forgotten to tell Mum I wouldn't be home for dinner. And I had completely forgotten about Rudy.

We pulled up outside the house. Mum's car was there, but the house was dark. Jordan's dad left the engine running while Jordan hauled out my bike and put it in the garage. He closed the garage door and took a piece of paper out of his pocket.

"Give me a ring, if you want," he said.

I looked down at the paper: *Jordan Vincent*, it said, and a phone number.

"Thanks, Jordan. For everything." I hugged him kind of awkwardly, feeling like I had an extra arm or something.

I waved from the porch as they drove away then turned towards the door. I had my hand on the knob when it opened in my hand. Mum and Rudy.

Rudy came squiggling out, his rear end wagging so much I thought it was going to disconnect itself and fly off like a space shuttle. He slurped at my hand, whining as if I'd been gone forever. Mum leaned against the door, staring at me, her eyes glinting in the lamplight.

"I'm sorry, Mum, I completely forgot to phone, but it was okay because my friend Jordan . . ." I spoke quickly to try to head off whatever storm was coming.

She held up her hand, like, stop-talking-or-else. I stopped talking.

"I come home," she said quietly, "and the dog is alone, hungry and needing to go out. I find no note, no message . . . nothing." Her lips tightened into a thin line. I squinted my eyes and I swear I was bracing myself as if a big wave was about to hit.

But all she said was, "Julie, come in. You're shivering."

Mum had fed Rudy and I guess let him out,

because there were no messes or anything. There was lasagna out on the table and some salad. I looked at Mum as she slowly scratched Rudy's head, watching me eat.

"I'm sorry, Mum," I said. She nodded.

Later we both got into pyjamas and Mum made a big bowl of popcorn. We watched funny videos on TV of people doing stupid stuff. One guy tried to ride down this little plywood ramp on a mountain bike and looped right back around, plopping on his head. Another guy was chasing a goose that ended up biting him you-know-where.

Mum and I laughed so hard we knocked the popcorn over and Rudy immediately pounced on it. He inhaled it without even chewing, I swear. Then he sucked up the crumbs like a vacuum cleaner.

About half an hour later he got gas – so bad it would have stripped wallpaper off the wall. Seriously. And he kept doing it. Whichever of us smelled it first would yell, "Take cover!" and we'd put our pyjama sleeves over our noses and breathe through them like we were sucking back the last oxygen on the planet.

I think I said something dumb like, "Gee, Rudy really loves your popcorn, Mum. What'd you put in it? Stinkweed?" and she whacked me with a pillow. I whacked her back, and Rudy got up, dancing around and farting. I swear I hadn't laughed so hard in ages.

CHAPTER ELEVEN

I got up with Mum the next day. I got up earlier, in fact, because I made her pancakes. I used the recipe she always uses and I think they turned out pretty well. By the time Mum came out, I had a stack on the table with maple syrup and butter and everything. I even had hot water for tea.

"Wow!" she said. I could tell she was pleased. She was grinning in this kind of goofy but nice way, and her eyes actually twinkled. I couldn't remember her looking like that for a long, long time. Not since Dad left.

We both ploughed into the pancakes, but I got up and down a lot, getting milk for her tea, syrup, more butter. I wanted her to feel special, you know?

Rudy's digestion problems had not improved (and it was kind of disgusting trying to eat – I actually gagged) so I put him outside where he yipped and scratched miserably outside the sliding glass doors. I closed the blind and put on nice music and we could hardly hear him after that.

Mum and I clinked glasses of milk. "To Rudy," I said.

"To Rudy," said my mum.

After Mum went to work, I went out and threw a ball for Rudy, hoping that some running around would loosen up whatever was causing the stench. When the phone rang in the kitchen, Rudy snapped at my feet as I ran to get it. It was Dad and, you know, for a second I thought about pulling a Megan and hanging up on him. But I didn't.

"Hi, baby," he said. I didn't say anything.

"Look, babe, I think you and I should go and see someone. Someone who helps kids with their problems . . ."

"Why? So *you* can talk? Because I'm not the one with the problem."

"We've been over this, Julie. Just stop pretending. It's not helping. Now, I haven't talked to your mother about this . . . This is between you and me, okay? Look, I'm trying here . . ."

"You're trying, Dad, but you're not listening. You don't listen to anyone. Not to Mum. Not to me." Rudy stared at me, his brown eyes filled with worry.

He's a very sensitive dog, you know.

"So you expect me to believe that Evie would do
. . . what? Smash her own stuff? I mean, come on,
Julie. Why would she do that?"

"I've been thinking about that," I said. "To get
me out of your life. And it worked, didn't it? You
believed her instead of me. Does she even know
you're still phoning me?"

When he didn't answer, I knew she didn't.

"You know what, Dad? You walked out on Mum
because of Evie. You bailed on our *family* because
of her. You know what I think? I think you made
a really, really stupid mistake and that *you know it*.
But don't worry, because Mum and I are doing fine
without you!"

I slammed down the phone.

How is it possible that the guy I once thought
of as a hero could suddenly seem so small and
puny to me? I mean, I remember going shopping
with him when I was little and we were walking in
the car park. I held on to his finger and my hand
was so small that his one finger was as big as my
whole hand.

Was this what growing up was? You suddenly
realised that your parents didn't know what they
were doing, either?

I went back outside and sat on the step. Rudy tucked himself under my arm, with his head on my lap. I don't know how long we sat there.

The air was still. The sun burned through the thick clouds until they broke off into shapes. One cloud morphed into a dolphin and swam away. Another became a ship and sailed across the sky. . .

Rudy and I had just eaten lunch when there was a knock at the door. I looked through the peephole and almost fainted with shock. Megan was there.

She was sweaty because she'd ridden her bike over. For once her hair didn't look so great – it was sticking to her head.

I opened the door slowly, not sure how to act. I didn't say anything, but Rudy pushed past my leg and put his head under Megan's hand. She kind of stared at this dog – the one who'd thrown up on her – but then she started scratching his head mechanically. Rudy groaned and leaned against her leg and that was it. Megan and I started laughing. Rudy has that effect on people.

I held the door open and Megan came inside, Rudy close behind. She sat on the couch, I flopped into an armchair and Rudy settled himself across her lap, his eyes closed to sleepy half-moons in a second.

"How've you been?" asked Megan.

"Umm, kind of the same. Some things are better, some things are way worse."

She nodded and we didn't say anything for a minute. "Kevin and I broke up," she said. "I broke up with him."

I could hardly believe my ears. "How come? I mean, I thought you were crazy about each other."

She sighed. "I don't know. I didn't like myself around him. And then what you said . . ." She stroked Rudy's ear. "I guess I just felt like I was playing house or something."

She looked at me. "I want us to be friends again, Jules. I miss you."

It's amazing how things change so fast. Like one minute I'm thinking Megan and I will never be friends again and the next minute we're best friends again. Sometimes life is confusing, but it's okay, you know?

I threw Rudy's tennis ball at her (I know, really mature) and it caught her on the arm and bounced off Rudy's head. He sat up, like, huh? Whazat?

"Point!" I shouted.

"Oh, no you don't," shrieked Megan. She pushed Rudy off her lap and dived after the ball, which had landed between the couch and cushions. When she lobbed it back at me, it grazed Mum's lamp, which wavered between falling and standing upright. I leaped over and steadied it and Megan gazed heavenward with an I-have-seen-my-death-and-lived expression.

I snatched the ball and headed for the sliding glass doors, where Rudy (of course) got jammed with me, then I ran shrieking to the other end of the backyard with Rudy nipping at my heels.

When Megan followed, laughing, we threw the ball back and forth, playing keep-the-ball-away-from-the-big-stupid-dog until Rudy had flecks of foam flying off his face. Disgusting, yet sad.

By the time we plopped down in the grass, breathing hard, Rudy was panting like a middle-aged guy who'd just taken up jogging.

"Geez, Rudy," I said. "Do you need me to call an ambulance or something?" And he leaned over and gave me a big, slurpy kiss right on the mouth.

"AAAaagghh!" I spat in the grass and wiped my mouth on my hand and Megan cracked up, holding her stomach and lying back in the grass, tears of laughter streaming down her face.

It was so good to be friends with Megan again. I told her she didn't need to break up with Kevin to be friends with me, but she said he was kind of getting on her nerves anyway, so that was okay. Besides, she and her family were going on holiday for the next two weeks.

I didn't tell her about meeting Jordan. I didn't want to start giggling about him, like we always did about boys in school. I wasn't sure how I felt about him. I mean, I was pretty much a mess every time he saw me, and he still liked me? I couldn't figure him out, you know? He probably just liked me as a friend anyway, so it didn't matter.

It was almost dinner time when Megan left. Rudy and I sat on the front step waving (me, anyway) as she rode away. When she turned to wave back, she veered towards a pole and I screamed, pointing. But she managed to swerve away at the last second.

"Can you please try to not kill yourself?" I shouted as she disappeared around the corner.

We were still sitting on the step when Mum drove up. I could tell before she even got out of the car that she'd had a bad day. She slammed the door and walked quickly up the front path.

"Hi, Mum," I said.

Rudy whined. It was almost as if he knew what

was coming. I guess I did, too. I just didn't want to know.

Mum glared at me. "I got a phone call from your father today. It seems there was a problem at his girlfriend's house last weekend." The way she said *girlfriend's house*, she could have been saying *nest of vipers* and it would have been the same.

"Oh?" I said, my stomach tightening.

Rudy kept whining softly and Mum glanced down at him irritably, then back at me. "Was there a problem, Julie?"

I nodded, my cheeks feeling hot. I felt guilty, you know? Even though I hadn't done anything, I still felt guilty.

"Were you ever going to tell me about this?" she asked.

"I . . . I thought I could handle it," I said.

"Julie, I'm your mother. I want to know if something is bothering you."

"But I didn't do it!" I said. "I tried to tell that to Dad, but he won't listen. You believe me, don't you?"

Mum didn't answer for a second. "I don't know what to think," she said. "But, if you didn't do it, why did you hide this from me?"

"I didn't want you to get mad at Dad," I said. But that wasn't all. I also felt kind of dirty, you know? As if somehow I'd been part of something disgusting. I didn't say that part. I don't know why.

Mum glared at me. "Maybe your dad deserves what he gets," she snapped. "All I've ever done is try to . . ." She stopped, closed her eyes and took a deep breath. "It doesn't matter. So, what's for dinner?"

I just kind of sat there, with my mouth hanging open. It had been my turn to make dinner and I had completely forgotten.

My mum's eyes literally bulged out of her head. "Julie! You forgot? I asked you to do one simple thing today and you *forgot*?"

"I'm sorry. I'll go right now . . ."

"NO!" said Mum. She opened the door and stomped into the house. "You stay here on the step, sitting comfortably, and I will go and make us both some dinner, even though I've been working *all day!*" Even in the house I could hear her.

"Mum, I said I'll . . ."

"Too late! If you'd wanted to help me, you should've done it *before* I got home. What did you do all day? Watch TV? Walk your dog? You couldn't fit dinner into your busy schedule?" I heard cupboards slamming.

I sank back down on the step, close to tears. Over what? Dinner? Sometimes I hated my mum. I tried so hard, but I could never seem to please her. I felt as if all I did was screw up.

Finally I got up, slammed open the front door and marched into the living room. Mum was glaring at me from the kitchen, where she had just opened a tin of tomatoes.

"Mum!"

She put up her hand to shut me up. "Don't you even start, miss," she said, her eyes narrowing. "I am still your mother and don't you forget it!"

"So I forget to make dinner and that makes me a terrible person?"

Mum turned back to the stove and dumped the tomatoes into a pan.

"You're not being fair," I said. Rudy stood by my side, quivering. "All *I* did was forget to make dinner, but *you're* . . ."

Mum came around the kitchen counter and walked towards me, her finger pointed, her eyes boring holes in me. "Get to your room."

"No! Why should I?"

"GET TO YOUR ROOM," she bellowed and grabbed my arm. I tried to yank it out of her grasp.

There's a blur . . . a flash of brown as the dog lunges at her. Jaws wrap around her thin arm. I see the teeth – long and yellow. I marvel at how long they are, but

98

THE PRESENT

they scare me with their wildness, too.

*I try to scream, NO, NO, NO, but no words come
out, no words at all.*

A drop of blood blossoms on her shirtsleeve.

I could hear him crying. His howls echoed in the garage like a lost child calling for its mother. I put the pillow over my ears, but I could still hear him. He was crying for me. He had only been trying to protect me.

Mum had stared at her bloody shirt, her eyes wide, then slowly pulled the sleeve up. One bloody puncture mark. Not much, but enough.

"He bit me." She said it as if she just couldn't believe it. "He bit me."

She had hauled him off by his collar out to the garage. He hadn't fought it. And now his cries were shattering me like splintering glass.

Some time in the middle of the night I left the house. Mum's light was still on in her room, but I made no noise. The street was silent. Even Rudy had stopped howling, as if he could sense I was coming.

The moon was half-full, coating everything in silver shadow. Stars were flung across the darkness like diamonds. Still there . . . even after everything.

I opened the door to the garage and I could sense where Rudy was without turning on the light.

I just held him. He was shivering, but not from the cold.

I held on to that dog for the rest of the night, sitting on the concrete floor. Usually I'm freaked out about spiders and getting bugs in my hair and stuff like that, but I didn't even think about it.

I woke up to the sound of Mum's car pulling out. Good riddance. That's how I felt. She was gone for the whole day.

I think I ate breakfast, but I really don't remember. I just remember how I felt. Numb doesn't even describe it, you know?

I went to visit Elizabeth later. I took Rudy. I couldn't leave him alone in the house. What if Mum came home and I wasn't there? I didn't know what she might do.

I took it slowly, because Rudy didn't seem to have much energy. It was as if he could still remember last night, you know? I didn't push him.

The air felt heavy, as though it pressed against my head. Thick, sticky-looking clouds swarmed overhead, but no rain.

The gravestones greeted us. Old friends – Willard, Isaac, Frances, Thomas. Rudy didn't pee on any graves. I knew I should be glad about that, but he wasn't acting normal.

At Elizabeth's grave, I sat and patted the ground for Rudy. He came and stood in front of me, his muzzle almost touching my nose. I looked into his eyes, the colour of earth and leaves and cool water . . .

"Lie down, buddy." He curled up next to me and settled his head on my lap and I stroked his ears and his eyes, so he had to close them. Finally, he fell asleep, and for once he didn't drool.

The clouds were gathering and my head felt like it was on too tight or something. I looked at the shadows moving across Elizabeth's grave marker.

"Elizabeth," I said, "I wonder if you had any problems like these. I mean, I know you were only little when you died, but I bet your mum didn't have problems she couldn't handle. Your dad didn't run off with someone else."

I felt like a whole world of sadness was trying

to squeeze out in tears that wouldn't stop, but I swallowed them back down.

I lifted Rudy's head off my lap, settled him on the grass, and I walked up and down the hill around Elizabeth's grave, gathering the tiny wild flowers that grew in the grass. I put half of them on her grave and laid the rest on the graves of her parents, John and Emily.

Then I sat, looking out over the hill, listening to Rudy snore softly. I could see the path to Jordan's house through the trees. I didn't know what to feel about Jordan. Part of me hated being around him, because I couldn't forget how messed up my life was compared to his. Another part of me loved being around him. He was really easy to talk to and how many guys could I say that about? Not even my dad.

It wasn't Jordan's fault he had the perfect life while mine stank.

I shook Rudy. "Come on, buddy. Let's go and visit Jordan."

We pushed down through the long grass and maples to Jordan's house. There weren't any cars in the driveway but that didn't mean he wasn't home. I remembered his saying that his mum Celeste worked as a nurse and Gerald worked with computers. Jordan's sister went to college full-time, so that meant he might be home alone with his nephew.

I rang the doorbell and Jordan opened the door so fast I kind of screamed.

He laughed. "Sorry, Julie. I just put Trevor down for a nap and I didn't want the doorbell to wake him up." He opened the door wide so I could get past. "What's up?"

"Oh, nothing," I said. "Just checking in with Elizabeth."

"Yeah? What is it with you and that kid?" he asked. He said it with a smile on his face, but it hurt my feelings a little, you know? Like he thought I was some kind of a freak. I just shrugged.

Rudy had made himself at home, stretching out in the middle of Jordan's living room like he was the king of Siam. I said something about needing to find a palm frond so I could fan him and Jordan laughed.

"So, what's up?" he asked again.

"Nothing. I just wanted to say hi," I said. "What's up with you?"

"Nothing," he said. "I get to look after my baby nephew all summer instead of going out with my friends." He flopped on the couch. "And you?"

I slouched in the armchair and didn't say anything.

"That bad, eh?"

"Last night Rudy bit my mum."

Jordan bolted upright, blinking, like I-must-have-heard-wrong. I nodded. "He was trying to protect me. Mum and I were fighting."

"What'd you do?"

I leaned back. "I didn't do anything. I just stood there. I remember seeing Rudy jump at her. He broke her skin."

Jordan shook his head. I swear he must have thought I had the most messed-up family, and I wouldn't have argued.

"And you know what else?" I said. "My dad's girlfriend threw around her stuff and broke it, really expensive stuff, like glass ornaments. Guess who she blamed?"

Jordan didn't say anything.

I went on. "Me. Of course she blamed me. Then she kicked me out. I even wrote my dad a letter saying how I didn't do it, but he didn't believe me." I closed my eyes. "I envy you so much."

"Why?"

"Because your life is so great. Your mum and dad are so cool. I mean, you guys talk to each other. You even seem to *like* each other."

Jordan didn't say anything for a second. "Julie," he said. I opened my eyes. He was staring at me with a funny expression on his face. "My life isn't so easy, either."

"Jordan, you don't even know how lucky you are. You have this perfect life, where people care about you and wonder where you are if you come home too late . . ."

Jordan stood up, looking upset. I knew I'd said something wrong, but I wasn't sure what. My head felt like it was being squeezed. I wished I'd never come over.

"You know, Julie . . ." He shook his head, licking his lips as if he'd tasted something bad. "You know, you come in here and look around for a minute and you decide I've got it made. Yeah, my family is great most of the time, but they aren't perfect, either. I wasn't asked if I wanted to stay home and take care of my sister's baby for the summer, I was *told* I was going to do it. I know she doesn't have the money to pay someone else, but still . . ."

His eyes softened and he knelt in front of me, putting his hand on the arm of the chair. "Julie, if your life is messed up, fix it. *You* fix *your* life."

He took my hand, but I yanked it back.

He looked shocked.

"I thought . . ." I said, shaking my head. "I *really* thought you would understand, but . . ." I bit my lip to keep from crying. Not here.

"Julie, I wasn't trying to be mean, I was just saying . . ." He reached for my hand again.

The ocean hammers against my skull. No safe place. Nowhere to go.

I pushed his hand away and scrabbled my way out of the armchair. "It was stupid of me to . . ." I headed for the door, Rudy beside me.

"Julie, wait. Don't go." From the bedroom, Trevor started to cry.

I went down the stairs. Up the path. On my bike, I pedalled. One foot and then the other, Rudy running beside me. Always beside me.

The phone was ringing when I got home. I ignored it. I fed Rudy and fell into bed, shutting the blinds to the afternoon light.

Ink fills my eyes, my nose . . . I breathe black liquid into my lungs and they burn. I turn around and around, swimming, struggling, scraping my hands through liquid so thick it congeals around me. I can't see . . . I can't see which way to swim . . .

THE PRESENT

CHAPTER THIRTEEN

Rudy was licking my face when I woke up. He gets nervous when I dream, you know? Maybe I scare him or I cry or whatever. Anyway, I woke up with dog slobber all over my face, so I got up to wash it off.

When I opened my door, Mum was standing right outside, like she'd been waiting for me. Her clothes were creased and her hair uncombed. She had a bandage where Rudy had bitten her. A purple bruise with yellow edges spread beneath it and across her arm.

"Have you found a home yet?" she asked.

I looked away down the hall. "Have I *what?*"

"Have you found a home yet?" She put a hand heavily on my shoulder. "For that dog?"

I shrugged off her hand. "Why?"

Her eyes widened and she leaned into me. "*Why?*"

she said. "Why? Because he . . . he . . ." She lifted her arm and stared at the bandage, frowning.

"He was protecting me," I said. "From you."

Her nostrils flared and her eyes narrowed. She turned and walked out of the house.

I scrambled a couple of eggs and ate on the back step. Rudy hadn't eaten yet and he sat down in front of me, wearing his you-never-feed-me look. I threw him half an egg.

What Jordan had said really hurt my feelings, but I couldn't even figure out why. Maybe it was because I thought he had it so good, but really he was just kind of brave, you know? So what did that make me?

He had said something like, it's your life, so you fix it. It upset me at the time. I guess I had just expected him to be my shoulder to cry on. But he was right. Trouble was, I didn't know what to do to fix it.

I got the phone and realised I didn't have Jordan's number on me, so I went through the dirty clothes on my bedroom floor until I found the pants I had been wearing the night he dropped me off. His phone number was still in the pocket.

When he answered, I opened my mouth to talk, but nothing came out. "Hello? Hello?" he said.

I hung up.

Rudy stared at me like you-are-an-idiot, so I pushed him away with my foot, but he came back and sat next to me, still staring.

"Now what?" I asked. His brown eyes were unblinking.

I redialled Jordan's number and he picked it up and said "Hello!" in a please-stop-bugging-me kind of voice.

"Hi," I said.

"Julie?"

"Yeah."

"Julie, I'm sorry I . . ."

"No." That's all I said. Just no.

I took a deep breath, and I could feel the ocean in the background, but I said no to that, too. I said, "Jordan, don't you dare be sorry. Because . . . I mean . . . You were right about everything."

Rudy sighed and sank to the ground, covering my feet with his soft fur. He closed his eyes and smacked his lips.

"I just . . ." I paused. "I just don't know how to *fix* it, you know?"

"You'll figure it out," he said.

I nodded, then realised he couldn't see that, so I said, "Yeah."

"Hey, are you going to be visiting Elizabeth any time soon?"

"I guess so."

"Ring me when you go. I'll come with you."

"Thanks."

"Trevor the Terror is awake so I've got to go, but ring me, okay?"

"Okay. Bye."

I scratched Rudy's ears. He's a smart dog.

I fed Rudy and threw the Frisbee for him for a while. I needed time to think about everything – what I was going to do. I worked with him on some tricks. He had forgotten the "Bang" one so we practised that until he was flopped on his back again, impersonating road kill. He knew how to shake hands, come, stay.

"Hey, we should go visit Evie again – destroy another of her desserts!" I was joking, but it wasn't such a bad idea. Only I'd leave Rudy at home.

I rang Dad's number. "Dad, it's Julie."

"Oh, you know, now isn't a good time, babe. Can I ring . . ."

"No, you can't ring me back. You're going to come and get me and take me to Evie's house."

"Now I told you that Evie said . . ."

"Put Evie on the phone."

There was silence. Dad covered the phone and I heard him talking and then Evie's voice, sounding angry. I couldn't make out what she was saying.

She got on the phone. "What do *you* want?"

"I'll tell you, Evie. I'm going to come over there and you, me and my dad are going to talk."

She laughed. "I don't think so, after what you . . ."

"Fine. I'll call the child protection services. See what they have to say about it." Evie didn't say anything, but I could hear her cat breath going in and out.

"Tell my dad to come and get me within the next fifteen minutes," I said, "or I'm phoning right now."

"Now, Julie, honey, calm down . . ."

"*Don't tell me what to do!* I'm hanging up and calling now . . ."

"NO!" she said. Then she gave this weird little laugh, like everything-is-just-fine. Dad must be listening. "Come on over then," she said sweetly.

Dad turned up, tyres squealing. I came out, but there were no tears of joy and running across the lawn in slow motion like in a bad movie. I got in the truck and slammed the door.

Dad took off so fast I smelled burning rubber. Oh, well. He could get new tyres for all I cared. He took the corners so fast we were nearly two-wheeling. I just hung on and enjoyed the view.

He lurched to a stop in front of Evie's little house of tortures, got out, slammed the door behind him and strode up the driveway. I noticed his hair was turning grey. Unmarried life didn't agree with him, I guess.

The pines towering over her house filled the air with a clean, honest smell that didn't go at all with the woman living under them. But it smelled good anyway.

When I got to the door, it was closed. How immature could two adults get? Maybe they thought I would go away because I was too afraid to open the door?

I admit, my heart was hammering a little, but I opened it. Evie was sitting on the couch. Dad was at the dining room table, his head in his hands.

"Well?" said Evie.

"Gee, you guys. No *Hi, Julie honey, how are you?* No *Please sit down?*"

Dad banged the table with his fist, without looking up.

"Say what you want to say to me and get out," said Evie, her green eyes glinting.

"Actually, Evie, I don't want to say anything to you." I walked over to my dad. "I'm here to talk to you, Dad."

He said nothing.

"You know what really happened, don't you? You know that I was telling the truth the whole time."

Dad looked up at me. "We've been over this, Julie . . ."

"Ask her why she let me come over," I said.

His back stiffened. "There's no need, I know what . . ."

"Honey, don't listen . . ." Evie started in at him.

"Ask her."

Dad looked towards Evie, not even moving his head, just his eyes. For a second, he didn't say anything. I was holding my breath. This was it. This was everything.

He said slowly, "Why *did* you let . . .?"

Evie gasped, "You're asking me? You don't believe

me now?" As if she'd never been so insulted in her life.

She got up from the couch, staring at my dad like a leopard stares at lunch, and practically flung her glass on the coffee table, where it wobbled and fell on to the carpet. Her face turned blood red, and I swear I wouldn't have been surprised to see her head shoot off her neck like a missile. My dad watched her, his mouth hanging open.

She wrenched open the front door and stood ramrod straight beside it. "GET OUT!" she screamed. "GET OUT OF MY HOUSE!"

Dad stood up slowly, shaking his head over and over again like I-want-to-wake-up-now.

Evie left her place by the door and flung open the coat cupboard, throwing his coats onto the floor, kicking at them with her tiny high-heeled feet. "AND TAKE YOUR STUFF WITH YOU!"

She attacked his clothes in the bedroom next, dumping them on the cute little puffball shrubs in the front lawn. They looked better out there, anyway.

"Evie," said my dad, holding out his hands towards her. "You lied?"

She froze, goggling at him. Then she laughed. "GET OUT! GET OUT, YOU IDIOT!"

CHAPTER FOURTEEN

Dad drove me back home without a word. Fat drops of rain began to spatter the windscreen and he stared through it with the empty-eyed shock of an abandoned child. We pulled up to the curb and he clenched the steering wheel with both hands.

"Dad?" I touched his hand.

He looked at the house. I could tell he wanted to walk in there as badly as I wanted him to. How can things get so messed up?

I took a deep breath. "Remember how you always promised you'd take me out for a coffee?"

He frowned, his eyebrows scrunched, and shook his head no.

"Yeah, I know, but you should have, so why not take me now? Please?"

Dad put the truck into gear and pulled away again. At a coffee shop near the supermarket we parked and got out. I hooked my arm through his and steered him inside.

"I hope you've got some money because I haven't," I said.

He looked at me, and for just a second I thought he smiled. He got out his wallet without a word.

I ordered for both of us and we sat at a table near the window, watching the people walk by, pushing their shopping trolleys. I blew on my hot chocolate. He stared at his coffee. Finally, I added some cream and two sugars, the way he likes it, but he just kept staring. I pushed the coffee towards him.

Slowly, he lifted it up and sipped it, smacking his lips a little and nodding. Then he blinked and shook his head like he was still trying to wake up.

I looked at him over my cup of hot chocolate – dark circles under his eyes, hair greying, cheeks sunken. There was no sparkle in his eyes, either. Just like Mum.

"Dad," I asked. "Why did you leave?"

He put down his coffee and shut his eyes. A tear slid down his nose and dripped onto the table, where it stayed. A tiny puddle.

"I . . . don't know," he said, his voice husky. "I . . ." His voice trailed off. He shook his head. More tears plopped into his coffee.

"Have you ever thought of talking to Mum about it?" I asked. He looked out the window – a million miles away, you know? Maybe he was thinking about some happy times with Mum? There had to be a few, didn't there?

He wiped his face with the back of his hand. "I don't want to talk about it with you, Julie."

I kind of blinked at him, like you've got to be kidding. I mean, I know he was hurting, but so was I.

"Why not?" I said. "Your girlfriend accused me of doing all sorts of stuff and you believed her. Now I'm trying to be mature about it and maybe help you and *you don't want to talk about it with me*?" My voice got kind of shrill and quavery. People started to stare.

"How about saying I'm sorry, Julie, for walking out on you. I'm sorry, Julie, for believing that woman over you. I'm sorry . . ."

"That's enough," said my dad, slamming the cup on the table. Hot coffee gushed out the top, scalding his hand, and he put it to his mouth, shaking his head and holding up his other hand to me like a police officer stopping traffic.

My face turned bright red and as we walked out of the coffee shop I swear I could feel every single person's eyes on my back.

We drove back home in silence.

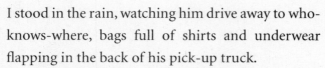

I stood in the rain, watching him drive away to who-knows-where, bags full of shirts and underwear flapping in the back of his pick-up truck.

It's weird but, even though I felt angry, I also felt sorry for him.

I opened the front door and listened. No sound. I sighed with relief until I realised Rudy hadn't met me. I quickly tiptoed in and shut the door. I looked on the couch. No Rudy. I looked down the hall. Mum's door was closed.

If Mum was asleep, Rudy had to be here somewhere. I mean, he couldn't grab the keys and drive himself to the edge of town. "Just calm down," I muttered to myself.

The hinges on my bedroom door squeaked like a haunted house. I crept up to the bed and patted the bed clothes, in case he was lurking under there. Nothing.

I listened outside Mum's door. There was a muffled snort and the sound of blankets rustling.

I stood in the hallway, my heart doing flip-flops. Something had happened to Rudy, I just knew it.

Suddenly, I heard him whine.

"Rudy?" I whispered.

He whined again and scratched at a door. He was trapped in the bathroom right next to where I was standing.

He whacked his head when I opened the bathroom door too fast, but he was too stupid to care. His tail was on wagging overdrive, and I swear I almost choked him to death I hugged him so hard. His eyes kind of bulged, but he managed to lick me pretty much all over my face. I didn't mind at all. I was so happy to see him.

"What were you doing in there, you stupid dog?" I said. "Did you drink toilet water and get trapped? It serves you right, you big dummy!" I buried my face in his fur. "I thought Mum had given you the chop, Rudy."

"You thought Mum had done what?"

Mum was standing in her doorway.

I got such a fright I screamed and Rudy winced, but I tried to laugh it off. "Oh, good morning, I mean afternoon. I didn't know . . ."

"Yes, I'm awake." She smiled, but it didn't reach her eyes. "You thought I had done what, Julie?"

For a split second, I felt so afraid, you know? I was kneeling on the floor, holding on to my dog and that's all I had. Just the floor and my dog.

Mum stood over me. She held out her hand towards me and I gazed at it in confusion until I realised she just wanted me to take her hand. I grabbed it and she pulled me up.

She didn't let go but looked into my eyes. "Tell me."

I stared down at my feet. The strap on my sandals was coming loose. I would need to get another pair soon.

"*Tell me.*"

"I thought you'd had him put down," I said slowly.

She let go of my hand. "I wouldn't do that, Julie. You know that."

"You mean he doesn't have to go? Oh, Mum, thank you! I swear he'll never do that . . ."

"I didn't say that." Her eyes didn't blink, but stared into mine. "He's going. But I would never put him to sleep without telling you. Without letting you say goodbye. I want you to know that." She looked away. "If you can find him another home, that's fine. But they'll have to know he's vicious . . ."

"He is *not*!" I said. "You know what happened. He thought you were going to hurt me."

She pointed at Rudy, her finger shaking. "That dog is dangerous and I will not have him in my house."

"It's *my* house, too," I said. "Rudy is part of this family."

"No," said Mum. "Not any more."

Anger flared up from my throat. "You're right!" I screamed. "Because there *is* no family."

Mum flinched. I went on. "You drove Dad away because he could never do anything right." I stopped, my breath coming in gasps. "But you know what else, Mum?" I said. "I'm *scared* of you. If you're such a great mum, then why am I afraid all the time?"

Mum stared at me, saying nothing, her lips shaking.

"You think you're the only one who's going through anything? You and Dad have completely forgotten about me. You only care about yourselves and your own stupid problems. It's pathetic that my *dog* cares about me more than you do!"

I looked at her like she was a bug. "I *hate* you."

Mum fell back against the wall as if she'd been struck. Her face crumpled slowly and she bowed her

head, tears dropping from her face, making dark, wet stains on the rug.

———

I watch the girl stumble away. I watch from the ceiling, where it is safe. I follow behind as she lurches down the hallway, holding on to her dog's collar. She throws open the front door and stumbles down the front stairs with her dog. They disappear down the street, into the dusk.

I see everything and I worry. I worry about that girl.

CHAPTER FIFTEEN

Car lights swerved in front of me, a horn blaring loudly. Rain spattered my face. I gazed around me. I wasn't even sure where I was. Houses lined the street, big trees leaning over them. I felt as if I should know this street but it was like I was looking through fog. I was so tired.

Something pulled my hand and I looked down. I was clutching Rudy's collar so tightly my knuckles glowed white under the street lamps. He pulled again, leading me. We walked to the end of the street to a two-storey white house with red shutters. It was Megan's house.

There was a car in the driveway and a light on in the living room. I banged on the door. No answer. I banged again, harder and longer this time.

"Megan!" I shouted, peering through the glass door. There was no movement inside. Just a light on to keep the burglars away, the way it was every summer when they went on holiday.

At that point, my legs just kind of gave out and I sank to the porch. Rudy stood beside me, gently whining, wagging his tail. Suddenly, he stiffened and I could see the fur on his back stand straight up.

He was staring at the road where a car was driving slowly past, its driver's face barely visible, but I could tell by the flash of white that, whoever the guy was, he was staring straight at me. The car went a little further and started to make a slow U-turn.

"Come on, Rudy," I whispered. I jumped off the porch and we ran for Megan's backyard as the car completed its turn. Rudy and I watched from behind the hedge as it drove slowly back. Rudy growled deep in his chest.

There was a sturdy-looking broken branch lying out on the lawn, in the open. When the car had passed, I ran out, slipping on the wet grass, and grabbed it. Back behind the hedge, my heart thundered in my ears.

I held the branch like a baseball bat. Rudy's lip was curled up and his teeth bared. If the psycho found us, he'd have way more than he could handle. Rudy and I would make sure of it.

The car drove back and forth a couple more

times before finally taking off. I felt all rubbery and shaky, but I couldn't just hide in Megan's backyard all night.

I waited another five minutes before we climbed out of the hedge. I was soaked. I had no idea where I was going or what I was going to do.

I kept a tight hold on the stick and Rudy and I slipped from bush to bush for a while until we were sure we weren't being followed. Whenever a car came, we hid behind something until it passed.

We walked back along the same road. There was a long stretch where there were no houses. Just some scattered trees and a deep ditch – the same one I'd fallen into what felt like years ago now.

The moon was covered in cloud, drizzle falling in a hazy curtain. My legs were bare. I thought it was probably safer to walk in the ditch and started down the bank. My stupid sandal chose that moment to finally break and I tripped and slid down on my butt, thumping against the other side of the ditch and scratching my leg on the stick.

I just kind of lay there for a second, thinking, you know, this can't be happening, please wake me up now. Rudy stood over me, his ears dripping, his dark eyes sad. Even in the weak moonlight, I could tell.

I dropped the stick and hauled myself up, only

one sandal on, and sloshed through the ditch. Rudy walked in front of me, turning every metre or so to make sure I was still following. When cars passed by, I lay against the bank so they couldn't see me. Rudy crouched right down, too.

When I saw the hill in the distance, I knew where I had been walking to this whole time.

I used a clump of weeds for a handhold and crawled out of the ditch. There were the tall maples that surrounded Jordan's house. The house was bathed in warm light, shining from its windows. They would help me. Jordan's family would take me in, give me a bath, dry clothes.

I walked up the little path edged with his mum's flowers and stood in front of the door, my hand raised to knock. I could see them in the living room. Jordan was stretched out on the floor, his hands behind his head, watching a movie. Celeste and Gerald sat on the couch, his arm around her shoulder. Sheree was reading a textbook at the kitchen table. It was late, so Trevor was probably in bed.

I realised my hand was still poised in mid-air, ready to knock, but I couldn't do it, you know? I couldn't make my problem their problem.

When I turned away from the door, Rudy looked at me like, huh?

"Come on," I said. And he did. Even though I knew he wanted to go in there as badly as I did.

We climbed up the hill. The rain was heavier now and little rivulets were flowing down my neck and back. It was dark. There were no street lights up there and the moon was hidden by cloud. Around the perimeter of the hill, the trees stood black and motionless. My foot slipped out of my one sandal and I fell hard on my knee. I patted the ground until I found the shoe and flung it down the hill. Better off without it.

We kept walking. The hill seemed bigger in the dark. The only sounds were of the rain spattering against the grass and Rudy's and my breathing. The lights of the cars below seemed like glowing, snaking worms, but they had no real relation to us. We were outside of the world. Outside of time.

The gravestones appeared out of the dark, jutting like broken teeth. Rudy started to whine.

I ignored him and threaded my way through the stones. Willard, Isaac, Frances, Thomas. I couldn't read their names in the dark, but I knew they were there. I reached Elizabeth.

"Hello," I said.

I sat next to her, hugging my knees for warmth and comfort. Rain dripped off my hair and into my eyes. I could just make out the outline of her gravestone. Two years old. That's all. Then she was gone.

Rudy sat in front of me, whining. He wouldn't stop whining.

"Stop it," I said.

Maybe he didn't understand me, because he kept doing it.

"Stop . . . *whining*," I said. I was very clear. But he wouldn't stop.

I breathed in slowly. I fought the feeling, but I really wanted to make him stop, you know? I just wanted him to shut up.

I breathed slowly and turned my attention back to the grave. "Elizabeth, I feel like you're my sister. I know it sounds stupid, but I feel like I know you somehow. You had the right to live and have a happy life, but you didn't have that."

Rudy hadn't stopped whining the whole time. I lost it. "RUDY!"

He cringed and backed away from me. For some reason that just made me angrier. "RUDY, JUST SHUT UP OR . . . OR I'LL . . . I'LL . . ."

I started to sob – great heaving sobs that felt like my whole insides were going to come out. I tore at the grass with my hands and pounded the dirt. Rudy came towards me.

I swung my arm and hit him, catching him behind the ear and knocking him to the ground. He yelped, scrambled to his feet and ran a few steps away. Then he just stood there, whimpering.

"SHUT UP!" I screamed. "JUST SHUT UP!" I ran at him with my hands balled up and he turned and ran, his tail tucked under, into the dark.

I stood breathing hard, my hands curled into hard fists. At last my breathing slowed and I was alone. It seemed as if everything in my life had led me to this moment. I was alone, I was shivering, but I didn't care.

I knelt on Elizabeth's grave, staring at the stone, glowing pale in the dark like a beacon. I lay over the grave, face up, eyes open, arms outstretched. Rain rushed towards me and I closed my eyes and opened my mouth to receive it. I was finished trying to fix what was broken.

The ocean washed over me . . . surging over the walls.

I watch from above. I see the girl, lying on the child's grave. She looks cold and pale and my tears shower from the sky, streaming down my own cold cheeks, for the girl.

I realise with a shock that I love her. I don't want to leave her alone any more. I reach down to hold her and gather her in my arms. And I feel the rain on my face, my legs, my outstretched arms.

The earth feels soft beneath me. Perfume from the soil fills my nostrils . . . the smell of rain on earth. I breathe deep, and hold on as the world spins.

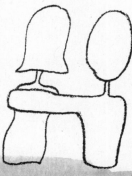

CHAPTER SIXTEEN

I lay in the rain a long time, until I finally noticed I was alone. I sat up, looking around for Rudy, and then I remembered. I got to my feet.

"Rudy!" I called, running among the gravestones. "Rudy!" I strained to see into the thick darkness. "Rudy, please come!" The rain fell so heavily I could hardly see a metre in front of me. I ran, traversing the hill, my bare feet sliding on the wet grass. "Rudy!"

I had hit him. But worse, for a split second I had hated him. And he had known, had felt it. My Rudy was gone, and I'd driven him away.

I ran, yelling his name, covered in mud and sodden grass, my wet hair clinging to my face.

Finally, at the far end of the hill, on the side furthest away from the graveyard, I found him. I couldn't see him and he didn't make a sound. But I just knew.

I walked steadily through the tall grass towards him. He didn't move, but I knew he was watching me. I stopped about two metres away and crouched down. "Rudy," I said. "Rudy."

He was hiding under a tall shrub, almost completely blended into the deep shadow. I knelt and crawled on my hands and knees under the bush with him. I didn't say anything, just pressed my face against his, stroking his damp fur.

I lay down under the branches, and opened my arms and he didn't even hesitate. He crawled into them. I held him, rocking him back and forth the way you do a baby. "I love you," I said, over and over. "I love you."

The rain stopped in the middle of the night. We slept under the shrub, holding on to each other. When I woke up, sunshine glinted off the drops of water, glimmering on the branches above us. My head rested on Rudy's back, I looked up, through the branches to the sky. It was so blue.

My clothes stuck to me as I crawled out from under the bush. Rudy was still lying down, his legs poking out sideways like four hairy sticks. He got to his feet, bumping his head against the branches and a cascade of drips fell on him. I laughed. I hardly even recognised the sound, you know? I didn't know what would happen or what I was going to do, but maybe things were going to be okay now. So I laughed.

Rudy barked at me, grinning. He was happy, too. I turned and ran across the open grass, with Rudy beside me, until I slipped and fell on my butt. It didn't actually hurt, just my pride, except when Rudy jumped on top of me.

He sat there, grinning and panting. A gob of his slobber fell down on my chin and I started to laugh because it was so gross. Then he licked me up one side of my face.

"You're a good dog, Rudy," I said. I scratched behind his ears, even though they were covered with mud.

There were a few wormy apple trees on the hill that must have been part of an old orchard and Rudy chomped on a few fallen apples, chewing them sideways as if he couldn't quite figure out how to eat them. One less-wormy apple was within my reach on one of the lower branches. It was still hard, but I bit into it anyway and spat it out again.

"Aagh! That is so . . ." Down the hill, a familiar

car was parked on the roadside. Mum.

For a second, I really didn't know what to do. The ocean lurched in my head and I just stood and breathed. Part of me thought, run. Another part of me thought that she wouldn't be here if she didn't, well, care, you know?

I couldn't tell if she was in the car. And I couldn't see her on the slope. I turned to look towards the graveyard and she was there, walking between the graves, her head turning from side to side as if she was searching for something.

Then she stopped and looked across the meadow as if she could feel me looking at her. She started to run towards me, then stopped, then started running again.

A cry welled up from inside me. "Mum!" I ran to her, my feet flying across the earth, and we hugged each other, holding on tight.

"Julie," she said. "Julie."

I squeezed my eyes shut, feeling her arms around me, knowing it was okay. It really was okay. Rudy stood to one side, with this forlorn look on his face, like, maybe they don't need me now.

"Rudy." Mum called to him. She let go of me and knelt in the grass, her arms wide. "Come here, boy." Rudy waggled over to her, his rear end threatening to fall off from wagging so hard, and licked all over her face and chin. "Yes, you are a good boy," she said. When she finally stood up, her jeans had wet circles at the knees.

"Mum," I said. "I didn't mean . . ." All of a sudden I couldn't talk. My throat got so tight, you know? All I could do was just look into her soft amber eyes. I couldn't remember really looking in her eyes before.

She laid her hand against my cheek. "Julie, you have nothing to apologise for. Everything you said to me was true. Everything. But one thing you need to know is how much I love you. Even when I screw up so badly and behave like . . ." A tear slid down her cheek. "I am so sorry for what I did. I won't ever . . ." Her face screwed up and she choked out, "I'll never leave you again. I promise." Her eyes were puffy and red and tears streamed down her cheeks, but I swear she'd never looked more beautiful to me. "Please . . . Come home?"

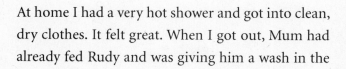

At home I had a very hot shower and got into clean, dry clothes. It felt great. When I got out, Mum had already fed Rudy and was giving him a wash in the bath. He jumped out and ran around the house, shaking himself and leaving behind a trail of puddles and wet hair. Mum chased him with a towel, saying, "Rudy, come! Rudy!" But she didn't seem to mind too much.

As I watched him run by for the millionth time, something occurred to me. "Mum," I said, "how did you know where to find me?"

She slumped into a chair, with Rudy just out of reach, panting and dripping on the carpet. She shook her head and rolled her eyes heavenwards.

"I saw your friend Jordan's phone number. You'd left it on the table. I phoned him early this morning and asked if he knew where you might be. He didn't want to say at first, but he finally told me about the little graveyard. He offered to go and look, but I wanted to do it." Mum got up and put the kettle on. "He sounds like a good friend, Julie."

I nodded. "He is."

"Why don't you invite him over for dinner?"

For the rest of that afternoon, Rudy and I played in the backyard and went swimming. I got him to do "Bang" and I could hear Mum laughing through the kitchen window.

That evening, Jordan rode over on his bike and the three of us sat down to roast chicken, homemade mashed potatoes, broccoli, beans and a cherry pie for dessert. Mum had been cooking all day and we had a real feast. You know, I really love her. She's not perfect, but who is?

After dinner she said that next time Jordan should bring his whole family over. They sounded like great people, she said, and I said, yeah, they were. Jordan and I helped clear the table and load the dishwasher and I threw the extra chicken meat into Rudy's bowl because I knew he'd love roast chicken as much as I do.

Mum said Jordan and I could take Rudy for a walk if we wanted, it was such a nice night. So we went out, and the stars were really bright. Like *really* bright.

Jordan pointed out constellations. "Look, there's Ursa Major. It's the shape of a bear. You see?" he said, pointing. "And Ursa Minor." He connected the dots in the sky for me with his index finger, but to me they still looked like dots.

"How can people see anything but stars?" I said. "I mean, how can you see bears and horses or whatever from just looking at the stars themselves?"

He shrugged. "I can. I like figuring out how they

all fit together." He gazed up at the sky with his mouth kind of hanging open, and I swear he looked just like a little kid who'd noticed the stars for the first time.

You know, I think that's what I like about Jordan. He's just himself.

"Hey, there's Cassiopeia . . ."

I followed where he was pointing, but I couldn't tell one star from another. Even Rudy stared up at the sky, looking back and forth, like he couldn't figure it out, either. I wondered if he even saw the stars? Anyway, he didn't seem to care one way or another, because he trotted ahead, panting and smiling, waiting for us to follow.

We started walking again, with Rudy in the lead, stopping every metre or so to make sure Jordan and I were following.

"Yes, we're right behind you, buddy," I'd say. In another two seconds, "Yep. Still here . . ."

Jordan walked Rudy and me back to the house and we all stood on the porch.

"Do you want a ride home?" I said. "I can go ask my mum?"

He shook his head. "I'm fine." He tucked a bit of my hair behind my ear and ran his finger along my chin. I swear my heart started beating like there was a jackhammer in there.

He smiled. "I really like you, Julie."

I blushed and couldn't think of anything to say, so I just stood there blushing. Rudy jammed himself between Jordan and me, not wanting to be left out.

Jordan leaned towards me and kissed me on my cheek. Long after he had gone home, I felt that kiss.

———

Rudy and I sat on the porch, thinking about everything. Or at least I was. Rudy was busy licking himself. I pointed out the constellations to him and you know he actually looked up.

"Can you see them, Rudy?" I asked. He blinked at the sky. And just for a second I think he actually saw them.

"They're always there, even when you can't see them. That's what's so amazing."

He looked at me as if to say, that-is-sooo-cool. I scratched him behind his ears. "I know. It is, isn't it?"

———

The moonlight plays in my room, making the shadows of branches dance across the wall. I lie in bed, my arms around Rudy, who smacks his lips and snores peacefully beside me. I'm just so grateful. For everything.

———

I stand at the top of a very high mountain. I gaze around me. Mountain ranges roll out before me like waves of a sea. I breathe deeply and smell wildflowers, ice and stars. I fill my lungs.

I look down at the dark, swirling ocean far below. I feel my feet slip, the rock crumbling, giving way, and I fall. I fall headfirst into the water's deep, gurgling ink centre and feel the cold shock. I remember I have been here before.

I hold my breath and swim. For a second, I do not know which way is up, and I swim frantically . . . this way . . . no, that way . . .

My lungs burn. I see a light above me. I push through the thick water that carries me upwards until I reach the surface. And I breathe.

EPILOGUE

Elizabeth's grave is in front of me. I touch the smooth stone, running my fingers along its top. Months have passed since I've been here. The daisies I left last time have either disintegrated or blown away. It's cold up here on the hill and I pull my jacket around me.

Jordan sits in the grass, not saying anything, just being with me. The cold doesn't seem to bother him. His coat is unzipped, as if it's a summer's day. But he's always like that. He strokes Rudy's head, who lies curled against his leg. Rudy's winter fur is wiry and thick, making him look even funnier than before. But that's okay.

I crouch in front of Elizabeth's grave marker and sweep off the dead leaves that have fallen around it. Why did I feel so much for this little girl who lived so long before I did? I mean she would have been dead by now, no matter what, you know? But I just did.

I think maybe it was because things were so bad back in the summer. I felt kind of like I was dead, too, you know? I mean, you know how bad things got.

I'm not sure how I feel about Mum and Dad. Dad's come over for dinner a few times in the last few months and they act like they want to try again. I mean, they both seem like they've changed. One part of me is really happy about that, I mean really happy. Another part of me is afraid it won't work out and it'll be like before.

But I believe people really can change, so who knows?

I pick up a bright red leaf and place it on her grave. I set a stone on top of it to keep the wind from carrying it away.

"Goodbye, Elizabeth."